Through Tears to TRIUMPH

Through Tears to TRIUMPH

God's Gracious Help
Through Grief and Sorrow

JOHN WALLACE STEPHENSON

Regular Baptist Press
1300 North Meacham Road
Schaumburg, Illinois 60173-4888

Library of Congress Cataloging-in-Publication Data

Stephenson, John Wallace, 1935–
    Through tears to triumph : God's gracious help through grief
and sorrow / John Wallace Stephenson.
        p.   cm.
    ISBN 0-87227-189-7
    1. Stephenson, John Wallace, 1935–   . 2. Widowers—Canada-
Religious life. 3. Bereavement. 4. Consolation. 5. Baptists-
Clergy—Canada—Biography.   I. Title.
BV4908.S74   1996
248.8'6—dc20   96-4075
                                                              CIP

Through Tears to Triumph
© 1996
Regular Baptist Press
Schaumburg, Illinois

Dedication

*To the hundreds of Christians who have
earnestly prayed for me in my grief*

and

*to those who are still struggling under
the weight of their own grief.*

Acknowledgments

The author would like to acknowledge the help and encouragement of the following people: Norm Maasdorp, Joyce Eaton, Wendell Kempton, Kristen Stagg and Jeannie Lockerbie.

Unless otherwise noted, all Biblical quotations are from the King James Version of the Bible.

The author and publisher would like to acknowledge the use of poetry from the following sources:

The poem on page 21 is from *Streams in the Desert* by Mrs. Charles E. Cowman. Published by Zondervan Publishing House, Grand Rapids, Michigan.

Poems on pages 33, 51, 65, 69 and 95 are from *When Loved Ones Are Called Home* by Herbert H. Wernecke. Published by Baker Book House. (Efforts to find the origins of these poems were unsuccessful. The publisher would appreciate any information concerning these sources and would be pleased to include them in any subsequent editions of this book.)

Poems on pages 59 and 77 are used by permission of Faith, Prayer and Tract League, Grand Rapids, Michigan.

The poem on page 62 is from "The Eternal Goodness" in *Treasury of Christian Verse*, compiled by Donald Kauffman and published in 1962 by Fleming H. Revell, a division of Baker Book House, Grand Rapids, Michigan.

The poem on page 83 is from the Quick Verse Selection of Bible Illustrator program. Parsons Technology.

The poem on page 89 is from *Toward Jerusalem* by Amy Carmichael. Used by permission of Christian Literature Crusade, Fort Washington, Pennsylvania.

Contents

Preface

Until recently, I was the least likely candidate to write a book on grief. As a pastor and missionary since 1962, I had often tried to comfort the bereaved. I never considered myself especially capable or able to speak from experience in encouraging those who were sorrowing. Lightning fast, however, my life changed dramatically. This is my story of how God graciously helped me through tears to triumph.

For months after the May 1993 car accident that killed my wife and daughter, I felt a deep need to write my thoughts and feelings and the Scripture passages that God was showing me in relation to healing my broken heart.

I began writing in November 1993, while I was in Cape Town, South Africa. I shared some of my articles with friends, Norm Maasdorp and Joyce Eaton, who encouraged me to continue.

In April 1994, on a visit to the headquarters of my mission, the Association of Baptists for World Evangelism (ABWE) in Harrisburg, Pennsylvania, I shared several articles with ABWE president Dr. Wendell Kempton. He told me to get writing: this story must be published. He also introduced me to Kristen Stagg, who greatly helped and challenged me to show, not tell, the message. In 1995 a gifted missionary writer, Jeannie Lockerbie, returned from Bangladesh to head up publications at the ABWE headquarters. She patiently and skillfully guided the editing to completion.

I have nothing but praise to God for His presence and power in my life while seeing me on this journey *Through Tears to Triumph*.

The Stephenson Family

Wally

Louise

David

Ruth

1

That Saturday in May

Shortly after midnight on Saturday, May 22, 1993, I was awakened by urgent knocking at the bedroom door of the home where I was staying during my speaking tour in the Atlantic provinces of Canada. A grave voice told me, "Someone just telephoned, and you are to call back right away!" I supposed that somebody needed pastoral counsel and/or comfort. Oh, how I disliked urgent phone calls in the middle of the night. Half asleep, I stumbled down to the kitchen to make the call where I wouldn't waken anyone else. The phone number belonged to my good friend Alex McCready! *What could be the matter? Had something happened to Alex's wife, Grace?* Mentally preparing myself, I dialed the number.

Alex picked up the phone on the first ring. "Sit down, Wally. I have terrible news. . . . Louise and Ruth were killed." The words struck me like bullets from an assault rifle, leaving a gaping hole in my heart. My brain froze instantly. Alex kindly gave me more information and prayed with me before hanging up. In unbelievable calmness, which could have come only from God, I made a number of phone calls to police and family. But my heart kept thinking, *No, no, it can't be true. This can't be happening! Louise and Ruth are really just at home.*

My mind flew back over the years to when I first met Louise. I had worked at Kodak in Toronto for four years after high school before going to the London Bible Institute in London, Ontario. Entering the halls of higher learning, I inquired at the business office where I might find a part-time job to help pay my way. I was told to see a student secretary who could give me the information I needed. I walked into the secretary's office and parked myself, as a farm boy would, on top of her desk. Louise never batted an eye at my unorthodox behavior. (She came from a farm background too.) We chatted about jobs, and in a few days I had one. Two months later I invited her to a hockey game, and that was the start of a great relationship—ended now by a tragic accident.

The previous evening I had telephoned Louise at our home in Burford, Ontario, about 75 miles southwest of Toronto. Louise knew that I was to meet Brian and Sheena Miller, who live in Lakeside, a suburb of Halifax, Nova Scotia, that Saturday afternoon. I was scheduled to speak in the Millers' church on Sunday morning and in a nearby church on Sunday evening. Up to that point on my speaking tour, I had immensely enjoyed meeting pastors and church members. I certainly did not enjoy being apart from my wife. But the trip was two-thirds over, and I was growing excited about returning home, especially since Saturday, May 22, was our thirty-third wedding anniversary. We were going to celebrate ten days late when I returned home.

Talking to Louise on the phone was a great joy and uplift to me. She was upbeat after having received good news regarding her health. She told me her plans: Alex and Grace McCready had come to visit. On Saturday Alex was going to clean up the front lawn where two large evergreen trees had been removed. Then, in the afternoon, Louise and our daughter, Ruth, would drive to Louise's mother's apartment in Oshawa, about 40 miles east of Toronto. They planned to stay overnight with Grandma and bring her back to Burford on Sunday afternoon for a week's visit.

Louise and I were scheduled to return on June 30 to our missionary service as interim pastor of Everglen Baptist Church in Cape

Town, South Africa, while fellow missionaries Dave and Julie Rudolph were home on furlough. Our house in Burford had not yet been rented for the time we would be in South Africa, but we knew God would work out this detail as He had thousands of previous ones. After talking about all these plans, Louise and I pledged our love and said good-bye. Ruth wanted to talk to me too.

Our only daughter, Ruth, an unmarried schoolteacher, lived in Guelph, about 50 miles west of Toronto, where she owned a home. She was excited as she updated me about her plans to go to Norway for six weeks as part of a team from our mission, the Association of Baptists for World Evangelism (ABWE), with international headquarters in Harrisburg, Pennsylvania. After her trip to Norway, Ruth planned to fly to California for her cousin's wedding.

Then the conversation took a more serious turn. Ruth questioned certain situations in the past and wondered how God was going to guide in her life in the future. We agreed that God did have a plan for her life and that He was in control. Then we made our cheery farewells. I could not have asked for a more happy, loving conversation.

As had been planned, at about 3:00 P.M. that Saturday afternoon, I arrived at my hosts' home. The Millers are a delightful young couple with three elementary-school-age boys. I helped Brian move some furniture that he had been given; then I joined the family for supper. Later Brian and I set up my slide projector/tape presentation at his church, and we visited one of Brian's friends. After we returned to the Millers' home, we chatted briefly; then I went to bed.

Back home in Burford that Saturday, Alex and Grace's visit and "Mission Front Lawn" had gone on as planned. In mid-afternoon, Louise and Ruth drove their own cars the one-hour trip to Ruth's house. They left Ruth's car there, and Louise drove our Oldsmobile Ciera. It takes almost two hours to get to Grandma's apartment in Oshawa. Louise telephoned her mother to say they planned to arrive in time for supper.

On highway 401 just east of Guelph, a car heading in the opposite direction was traveling about 70 mph when the driver fell asleep. His car veered across the narrow grass median and appeared slightly airborne as it struck our car near the driver's door. The outcome: Code 4—death at the scene. Death came instantaneously for both

15

Louise and Ruth; they did not suffer at all.

Some hours after the accident, a policeman arrived at our home in Burford to try to locate me. He spoke to our friend Nick Chosen, who had also worked on the front lawn. They went inside but could not locate my itinerary. Louise had not posted it in its usual place on the refrigerator. After futile searching, Nick made contact with Alex, who had a copy. It was then that Alex awakened me from sleep with his urgent phone call.

After speaking with Alex, I spent the remainder of the night in numbness and disbelief. My emotions were frozen, except for the occasional soft whimpers that escaped from my throat. Brian and Sheena quietly did all they could to help, including arranging a flight home. We prayed and read several psalms. "I will lift up mine eyes unto the hills, from whence cometh my help. My help cometh from the LORD" (Ps. 121:1, 2). "The LORD upholdeth all that fall, and raises up all those that are bowed down. . . . The LORD is nigh unto all them that call upon him" (Ps. 145:14, 18).

Waiting for morning, I lay on a couch in the living room with only a little light from the kitchen straying in. Events and segments of our lives together flashed on the screen of my mind. I remembered when Ruth was born in Exeter, Ontario, on August 29, 1963. A nurse held her up to the window of the hospital nursery, and even my unprejudiced eye could see that she was the most beautiful little girl ever born. With her big blue eyes set wide apart and her chubby cheeks, Ruth was a marvelously formed eight pounds and fifteen ounces. I was so proud of this little gift from God. I was sure I detected a faint smile from Ruth for her daddy— it was impossible that now she was dead!

At 6:00 A.M. on Sunday, May 23, Brian drove me to the church to pick up my equipment and then to the Halifax airport to catch a flight to Toronto. I do not know if Brian had tipped off the fellow at the counter, but he was extra courteous and helpful. I went through airport security and sat in a waiting area. Crowds of people surrounded me, but I felt as if I were the only person on earth.

On the two-hour flight, terribly bereft, I stared out the window at the clouds. As the Boeing 737 sped on, I sat like a stone. I had been looking forward to preaching that day, getting home in ten days, belatedly celebrating our anniversary, then heading for South Africa in forty days. My plans were shattered. I felt as if God had led me out on a limb of service for Him and then cut the limb off behind me. I was immediately ashamed of myself for thinking that, but my heart hurt so much and I felt forsaken.

Fellow mission friends, Reg and Helen Snell, and my brother Al and his wife, Gail, met my plane in Toronto. Al and Gail took me to Ruth's house where, after a number of futile attempts, I was finally able to contact our twenty-seven-year-old son, David, in Victoria, British Columbia. Since attending university and going out into the work world, David had lived away from home. I broke the tragic news to him as gently as I could, trying to help him with his loss. I knew he was devastated. He had enjoyed such a close, special relationship with his mother. Talking with David, I realized I wasn't the only one hurting. Our only other child was also crushed in grief, and I had to help him. With this burden I returned to our memory-filled home. David arrived the following morning.

The house in Burford was a beehive of activity, yet a haven of comforting, praying friends and family. A support team stayed with me twenty-four hours a day for several days. The mission sent Rev. Mel Cuthbert to minister to me. His first wife, Dorothy, had been killed in a car accident in São Paulo, Brazil, in 1974. I received tremendous empathy from Mel. No one understands as well as a person who has had a similar experience.

Dale Renout, pastor of our church in Burford, and Don Perkins, my long-term pastor friend from Bible school days, helped me plan the funeral. I gave some input, but I wasn't really there. Everything seemed a blur of people and motion. Only when I was alone in the quietness of my bedroom did my emotions start to thaw and tears gush.

We held the viewing on Tuesday afternoon and evening at Fellowship Baptist Church in Burford, where I had pastored for six years immediately prior to starting our missionary career in 1991. During that horrendous week, hundreds of people came to express their sympathy, prayers and concern. I was overwhelmed by the outpouring of love.

The funeral was conducted on Wednesday afternoon. Louise had been teaching prekindergarten at Central Baptist Academy of Brantford, Ontario, and Ruth had taught sixth grade for one year at the same school, so I chose to hold the funeral service at Central Baptist Church. Approximately 800 people attended. Don Perkins preached from the book of Job. He stressed the points that God knew Job and Job knew God. Then he asked those assembled, "Do you know God, and does God know you?" My greatest desire was that God would be made real to both believers and unbelievers. A number of Christian leaders who had worked with and had known Louise and Ruth testified of their genuine faith in action. God gave me the strength to stand and spontaneously express, without breaking down, my gratitude to the assembled friends for their love and prayers. I knew I was being carried along by God. With the congregation, I joined in triumphantly singing the concluding hymn, "How Great Thou Art."

On Thursday morning, we held a private family interment at the Pioneer Cemetery in Burford. Pastor Dale read Scripture passages focusing on our hope of the Resurrection, such as Jesus' words in John 11:25: "I am the resurrection, and the life: he that believeth in me, though he were dead, yet shall he live." Walking back to the car from the graveside, I experienced the most overwhelming sense of loss I had ever known. A gut-wrenching emptiness seized me like a gigantic vise, squeezing me until I almost fainted. I had said my final good-byes to Louise and Ruth. I was thunderstruck by the finality of death. My two vivacious ladies lay silent beneath the sod. We are separated for now, but not for eternity.

With the funeral over and the crowds gone, I started the long, slow road back to a new normality. I wanted then—and still want—to walk triumphantly through the valley of grief and adjustment. With His help, God and I will make it happen. I never doubted that I would return to Cape Town as originally planned, and I flew out of Toronto on September 2, 1993.

I marvel at how God upholds us through tragedy. Within two weeks of the funeral, I resumed my speaking schedule. I was able to go through personal effects, meet people and carry out duties in a satisfactory way. God helped me in ways "exceedingly abundantly above all" that I could ask or think. In addition to this enabling, I knew the power of the heartfelt prayers of hundreds of God's people. Even two years later, friends and even strangers speak to me or send cards and letters assuring me of their prayers. Recently I had a card from a lady in her nineties who told me that she prays for me daily. I am deeply humbled by such encouragement.

God's Word has been my constant consolation and companion.

It has been a "lamp unto my feet, and a light unto my path" (Ps. 119:105) during this horrific storm in my life. I have discovered afresh God's wonderful, sufficient grace in the deepest of trials. I know through experience that God will not put us through more than we can bear. I am learning the reality of the words, "I can do all things through Christ which strengtheneth me" (Phil. 4:13) in the process of moving through tears to triumph.

2

Coping with Shock and Numbness

I have been through the valley of weeping,
The valley of sorrow and pain;
But the "God of all comfort" was with me,
At hand to uphold and sustain.

—*Mrs. Charles E. Cowman*

For the first five days after receiving the news of the accident, I was in a state of shock. Webster defines shock as "something that jars the mind or emotions as if with a violent, unexpected blow." The effects may include lethargy, dullness and bewilderment. I was functioning, but as if I were operating in low gear. The Lord was merciful in preventing my "motor" from racing out of control. He installed the "governor" of shock and numbness to slow down my system until I was better able to cope with life.

Instead of tackling my daily routine, as I normally do, I had all I could do to get myself out of bed and dressed each morning. My mental processes were so retarded that I could scarcely decide what to eat for breakfast. I am thankful for friends who, every day for a week, placed a bowl of cereal or plate of toast in front of me without my having to think: *What will I eat today?*

Even when death is expected, the survivors feel the impact of shock. The finality of death often hits hard, varying in degree according to the personality of the survivor and his relationship to the deceased. Muscular weakness, upset stomach and tightness in the throat may be expected. As I stumbled through my first bewildering days alone, I clung to the daily reminders from God's Word that God cares for me and that He works all things together for His good, as He promises in Romans 8:28. Although I did not know how any good could come from what was then so awful, I knew this promise is true. God does not lie.

The numbness I experienced was not the physical paralysis that follows neurological damage, but more a sense of being anesthetized and unable to think as clearly or respond as quickly as usual. It is the same sort of sensation experienced when you see a car bearing down on you. You freeze in helplessness, unable to move. Everything seems to happen in slow motion. When people asked even simple questions, my brain, like an overloaded computer, slowly dragged up the information needed to respond. I shook hands with well-wishers, but shock acted like a dose of sleeping medicine, and I could not recall whom I had seen from one day to the next.

One of the first tasks following the death of a loved one is notifying family and friends. My brain wasn't thinking swiftly, but it was working well enough to keep asking, "Did anyone notify so and so?" Because the accident was reported through local radio, newspapers and television, almost all our local friends were aware of it and didn't need a phone call. Church and mission networking and word of mouth spread the news from California to Cape Town, from Norway to Bangladesh. As a result I had very few people to inform.

The details people wanted to know concerning the deaths fascinated me. What models of cars were involved? Were Louise and Ruth wearing seat belts? (Yes.) Would air bags have saved them? (I don't know.) May I suggest to friends of grievers that you restrain your curiosity for details. Someone grieving and in a state of shock is not the person to ask a lot of peripheral and hypothetical questions.

The second important task was to plan the funeral. I am a great one to talk on this subject! I had absolutely nothing planned. In a state of shock and intense emotional upheaval, my brain was barely functional. These conditions are hardly conducive to planning a funeral. Sometimes we have no choice, but most often we could do some preliminary planning. Sound morbid? Perhaps, but doesn't God want us to do everything decently and orderly, as we read in 1 Corinthians 14:40.

The first consideration is choosing a funeral home. Spouses should have an understanding with each other as to the funeral home of choice. Single and widowed adults could advise a family member or friend. Funeral directors offer choices, such as style of casket or type of funeral service, whether in the funeral chapel or in a church. I must warn the uninitiated that they are in for severe shock over the cost of funerals. Some people choose to plan and pay for their own funeral well in advance. Funeral homes offer lay-away plans (their pun). While some people cringe at the thought of planning and paying for their funeral ahead of time, I think that prepaying is considerate to the survivors; besides, preplanning allows for making choices for the funeral and burial.

In choosing a cemetery I had to decide quickly. I met a member of a local cemetery board on-site. We tramped around in the rain, looking at available plots, and I selected three plots together. I was amused to learn that cemeteries require payment before they begin digging. Even cemeteries have to face the reality of an uncertain economy!

Decisions to be made include the question of whether to bury or cremate, death/funeral notification in newspapers, public or private interment, memorial service or funeral service, viewing and visiting hours, burial clothes and cosmetics. For the funeral service itself, one must decide on the pastor(s), music, hymns, speakers, musicians, Scripture passages, pallbearers, and flowers or memorial donations to a charity. These details are a lot to think about when you are not in the mood to make decisions. I strongly advocate planning in advance. Planning prevents a great deal of emotional stress for the survivors. As a result of being unprepared then, I have given some thought to the matter. If I die before the Lord comes, I want someone to sing "Amazing Grace" and "How Great Thou Art" at my funeral, and I want the pastor to include the "Romans Road" plan of salvation in his remarks. Take the advice from the motto of the Boy Scouts, in which I participated as a boy: "Be Prepared."

During this state of shock, I received hundreds of telephone calls, cards and visits. Many sought to comfort me. The English word "comfort" suggests easing, soothing, relieving, cheering, moderating, strengthening and inspiring with hope one who, like me, has suffered great loss. The prayers of Christians play a vital role in comforting, as does the presence of family and friends with their encouraging words and thoughtful deeds. Many people were kind and thoughtful. They shed tears and hugged me or shook my hand firmly as if to say, "We love you, hurt with you and are standing with you." Some struggled to speak, but were unable to. All those people sought to comfort me with their words and presence. May God bless all their efforts. I will never forget the intensity of love on their faces. I was deeply moved by the unselfish deeds of both friends and strangers.

Some of the cards I received quoted 2 Corinthians 1:3 and 4: "Blessed be God, even the Father of our Lord Jesus Christ, the Father of mercies, and the God of all comfort; who comforteth us in all our tribulation. . . ." I read those verses repeatedly. The card that summed it best for me was signed with love and the words, "Only God can comfort you." How true that statement is! In bereavement, grief reaches a level that even the dearest friend in the world cannot touch. Only God can comfort and heal at that deep level. Isaiah 51:12 reads, "I, even I, am he that comforteth you." Chapter 66, verse 13, states, "As one whom his mother comforteth, so will I comfort you." When we hurt, God knows and feels it. Like a mother comforting her child who has scraped a knee or been viciously teased, God ministers to us in every area of need. As a wounded child flees to his mother, we can rush to the side of our Heavenly Father for comfort and help.

The word "comfort" in the New Testament means "to come alongside and help." Jesus used a form of this word in John 14:16: "And I will pray the Father, and he will give you another Comforter, that he may abide with you for ever." In answer to Jesus' prayer, God sent His Holy Spirit to comfort and help His people. If He is allowed to do so, the Holy Spirit will administer to us the power of Almighty God Himself anytime, anywhere and especially during crises such as shock and numbness.

"Who comforts us in all our tribulation. . . ." In every affliction, trouble or trial, God is able to comfort and aid us. Not a single situation in our lives is beyond God's care. In the midst of trouble it is easy to forget that fact and to allow self-pity to reign.

I have seen God comforting and helping His people in a myriad of troubles: Christian parents whose son was burned to death, a couple whose beautiful child died just a few days after birth, husbands whose wives died of cancer, wives whose husbands died of heart attacks, young couples who lost their hard-earned homes in an interest rate crisis, victims of traffic and industrial accidents, spouses who separated, business people whose partners absconded with company funds, men who lost their businesses in the recession of the early 1990s. In each case, God encouraged and helped His children to rebuild their lives. He comforted others. He is comforting me. And He will comfort *you* in all of your troubles.

As a friend of a mourner, be aware that your friend may be in a state of shock. Don't rush him to make decisions during this emotionally draining time. I am thankful that my family and friends did not badger me. I did not need someone talking incessantly, saying whatever came into his head, or quoting endless Bible verses.

Assure your grieving friend of your love, prayers and availability to help in any way. Demonstrate your concern by preparing meals. Help the griever make it through the daily routine, running errands or slipping him a piece of hard candy to relieve the tightness in his throat. Remember the words of Proverbs 15:23: ". . . A word spoken in due season, how good is it!" A few carefully chosen words, such as "We love you and are praying for you," or "Leave that to me; I'll take care of it" (then do it!), will be most helpful. Even a silent, comforting presence is appreciated.

3

Releasing Emotions

Weep your tears—
Suppressed, grief builds a dam
But spilled, it flows as a cleansing stream.
Grief is a cloud that appears:
Weep your tears.

Our eyes release the misery
The heart would store:
They see through heaven's veiled door
Death's victim win victory.

Weep your tears—
The loss leaves lesser pain
When faith reveals your loved one's gain.

Let peace dissolve all fears:
Weep your tears.
　　　　—God Gave You Tears *by Jean M. Wyness*

When Alex told me that Louise and Ruth had been killed, my emotions ceased functioning. I became a zombie. Robot-like, I gathered my clothes and stuffed them into my suitcases. Somehow my equipment was packed into cases for the trip home; I am foggy about how the packing was accomplished. Not until I reached the privacy of my own home, and especially my bedroom, did I feel free to express my emotions in a safe environment. I had not consciously tried to repress my emotions, because I believe that the expression of emotion is both necessary and good. But I was in a state of animated suspension. When my emotions were released, it was like a tire being slashed and all the air rushing out, concluding with intermittent puffs of air.

Releasing my pent-up emotions was a cleansing experience. It was as if someone had removed dirty bandages from a deep wound and had applied a clean dressing. Each subsequent emotional release was therapeutic and less painful than the previous one. The controlled, solitary release of my emotions greatly helped me.

In the first few weeks of grief, this release occurred almost every morning. That is the time I normally have my devotions, and I am more meditative and reflective then. The intensity and frequency of this emotional expression slowly decreased to the occasional occurrence.

Shedding tears and weeping are normal. The fact that I released my emotions does not mean I got hysterical or lost control. But allowing emotions to flow naturally is a necessary function in the healing process. Had I ignored or denied my emotions, I would later have been forced to confront my feelings in a far more painful manner.

The verse "Jesus wept" (John 11:35) is one of the most touching statements in Scripture. Here God the Son unpretentiously showed His humanity. God in tears—what a sight! Picture the scene. Jesus, walking into Bethany, met Mary and her friends. All of them were weeping over Lazarus's death. Jesus "groaned in the spirit, and was troubled." Then "Jesus wept." His tears flowed freely and unashamedly. Some bystanders observed, "Behold how he loved him!"

What does Jesus' weeping mean to me or you when a loved one dies? Jesus is not cold or uncaring. He sees our tears and is moved, perfectly sympathizing with our sorrow. If God can cry, so can a "keep-your-chin-up" man. In my times of tears, I sense the presence of my Lord silently weeping with me. I feel a bond in grief with the One who is a "man of sorrows, and acquainted with grief" (Isa. 53:3). I am not alone. He cares. My tears are not symbols of weakness. My faith is strengthened, and my innermost being is renewed with hope. I see the reality of my divine Role Model, who told us to "weep with them that weep" (Rom. 12:15). I am mightily encouraged by "Jesus wept." These words first challenge me to feel the heart sobs of those going through sorrow and then spur me to try to help them.

Most of us are not good at weeping; our society works against this kind of empathy. May I follow Christ's example for the glory of God.

My son's emotions were also in a high state of grief over the loss of his mother and sister. When a family suffers the loss of any of its members, each survivor has his own grief to bear, as well as the need to support the other members. Each of us reacts differently in any given situation, including the death of a family member. I was grieving and dealing with my own emotions, but at the same time I had a responsibility to my son, David.

My heart went out to David. It was hard for me to see him suffering. He and his mother had been very close. They shared a love for games. They played backgammon, checkers or other competitive pursuits by the hour. Over and over I would hear the loser plead, "Just one more game!"

Ruthie and her younger brother were typical siblings, fiercely protecting each other yet sometimes getting in each other's hair. Ruth was a little mother, and David, like most boys, didn't appreciate the attention. Losing his mother and sister was devastating for David. I prayed daily for his emotional healing. Three weeks after the accident, David returned to his home in Victoria, British Columbia. He became reclusive, overly tired and withdrawn in an attempt to avoid his grief. At the first Christmas after the accident, he allowed himself to feel the pain of his loss. He spent weeks remembering, reflecting and grieving intensely. After weathering this storm, David is rebuilding his life without his mother and sister. Remarkably, he has shown no bitterness toward God or others.

As David's father, I was in this crucible with him, and we developed a special bond. "How are you doing?" highlighted most of our telephone conversations. We found it beneficial to talk over our feelings and share with someone who was a partner in grief. This therapy was expensive, for part of the time I was in Cape Town, South Africa, while David remained in Canada! Even over the telephone, however, we were able to accomplish a great deal of emotional healing by talking things out.

In a family where death occurs, each member deals with his emotions and grieves individually as well as collectively. We should respect one another's unique ways of sorrowing. Before returning to the West Coast, David was helped by visiting the cemetery. I found taking a long walk more therapeutic. At the same time, we found mutual support in each other. I felt accountable to my son, and he to me. And we were not the only ones mourning. Louise's mother, brothers and sisters, in-laws, work associates and friends were also grieving. My hurt was so deep that I felt unable to help others much, but I trust that the strength God graciously gave me was an inspiration to my fellow-sorrowers.

When I arrived in Cape Town on September 4, 1993, functioning alone for the first time overseas where I was accustomed to Louise's presence, I might very well have had a nervous breakdown had I suppressed my emotions. Although Louise's absence was markedly evident as I unpacked my jumbled suitcases, which she used to pack so neatly, my life would have been far worse had I bottled up my loneliness and longings until they exploded, causing harm to myself, or worse, to the South Africans I was ministering to.

By now I think that I have passed through the majority of emotional white-water rapids. I still sail into an occasional turbulence, however, as a stranger innocently asks, "Where is your wife?" or "Do you have children?" In response I recount the sad story of their deaths. Depending on the person and the circumstances, I gauge how much detail to mention. I call this "reliving" the deaths. After such a conversation, when I am in private, my emotions may well up and release, not with the same intensity as immediately following the accident, but they well up nevertheless. I know people do not deliberately seek to hurt me with their questions, and I do not try to avoid answering them. I want people to talk about Louise and Ruth in a natural manner without evading the issue, but I feel the sting once again.

I learned that days and weeks would go by without a significant display of emotion, and I would think, *Aha! I am recovering,* only to find myself driving down some street, suddenly stabbed with sorrow, as if they had been killed only yesterday. But that, too, is part of recovery. These episodes might occur for the remainder of my life. The anniversary of the deaths and special occasions such as birthdays will certainly be times of emotional upheaval, but even everyday events can bring back the sorrow with great intensity. I find myself choking up when I see a young woman driving a red sports car like Ruth's, or when I see a mother and daughter shopping and obviously enjoying each other's company.

At the time of the funeral, I read Psalm 103:14: "For he knoweth our frame; and remembereth that we are dust." What consolation I experienced in knowing that Jesus understands me. In His compassion He knows my hurting heart and tender emotions. He understands the emotional upheaval in my life. There is nothing as reassuring as knowing that Jesus loves me.

The three most profound words in the world are "Jesus loves me." The Bible states that nothing can separate me from His love. In my hours of deepest grief, I could not escape the fact that Jesus loves me and will love me into eternity. What an anchor in the midst of a stormy emotional experience! That thought gave me an assurance and peace of mind beyond human understanding. I cannot imagine going through this upheaval as an unbeliever, who does not have the stabilizing effect of God's love.

Encourage the bereaved person to deal with his emotions, not by repressing them or engaging in self-pity. Identify with the Biblical examples of grief in seeking to express emotion in a God-honoring fashion.

We read in the Old Testament, "So Sarah died in . . . Hebron . . . : and Abraham came to mourn for Sarah, and to weep for her" (Gen. 23:2). Jacob "rent his clothes, and put sackcloth [on] . . . and mourned for his son [Joseph] many days" (Gen. 37:34). "David lamented . . . over Saul and over Jonathan his son" (2 Sam. 1:17).

In the New Testament, Acts 8:2 states, "And devout men carried Stephen to his burial, and made great lamentation over him." After Christ's crucifixion, the disciples mourned. Mary Magdalene ". . . went and told them that had been with him, as they mourned and wept" (Mark 16:10).

As the friend of someone who has lost a loved one, recognize that the griever has emotions that may erupt unpredictably and with varying intensity from a gentle trickle to a powerful geyser. This emotional eruption is especially true immediately following the death of the loved one. Be sensitive to the fact that your friend is on an emotional roller coaster.

Don't badger your friend to "snap out of it" because you are uncomfortable seeing his raw emotions or because you think his suffering has gone on long enough. Allow him to express his feelings without judgment. Keep Kleenex® at hand for your friend's use when he chokes up. Don't look aghast, but place a reaffirming hand on his shoulder and give him a reassuring "It's OK" smile. Be prepared for inexplicable outbursts of tears, anger or the doldrums as your friend progresses through the stages of loss. Be patient. Reaffirm your love. Include in your conversation praise and adoration of God and His attributes and deeds.

4

Facing Reality

I cannot think of them as dead
Who walk with me no more;
Along the path of life I tread
They have but gone before.
—Frederick Hosmer

I believed the devastating news of Louise's and Ruth's deaths, which my good friend Alex told me. I believed the facts that the investigating police officer gave me. Yet none of it seemed real. I felt as if I had been caught in the middle of a nightmare. It simply could not be true!

I was not denying reality; my head knew that the facts were as I had been told, but my heart wanted to believe that all was as it had been and that we would be together again soon. Louise and Ruth had just gone shopping; they would be back home in due time. These sentiments were especially prevalent until the burial service. When I stood at the graveside, transfixed in grief, the truth slowly penetrated. The incredible relationship forged with Louise over thirty-five years had been torn from me in a second of time. I walked away, shaking my head. I almost had to pinch myself to be sure I was not dreaming.

In the three months between the accident and my departure

for South Africa, I saw Louise and Ruth everywhere. Like mirages, they were as they always had been: Louise, arranging lilacs in a vase or crocheting a colorful afghan; Ruth, telephoning each evening for a little chat. I could hear their cars pulling into the driveway. It was time for Louise to be cooking dinner, but where was she? Ruth always called if she was going to be late, but the phone was not ringing. In each instance, reality brutally stated, "They are dead now." The battle between reality and my desires had begun.

As I packed and prepared to fly back to Cape Town, South Africa, for seven months as pastor of Everglen Church, I was beset by uncertainty at the implications and problems of being alone as a missionary. Louise had always been my partner in ministry. I thought, *I can't be going alone. I can't do this without Louise. It's not right. It's unreal.*

Packing, flying from Toronto to Heathrow and on to Cape Town, and settling in at the Rudolph home while they were in the United States were troublesome, but this time could have been far more difficult. God provided friends and family to help at every stage. I am not as organized as Louise was. She took care of packing the luggage. Trying to fit my clothes, shoes, books and toiletries into suitcases was frustrating. Louise's packing methods had managed to keep my suits virtually crease-free, but my work resulted in a crumpled mess. And how had she managed to fit in so much stuff? I could get only about half as much in as I remembered Louise cramming into our bags.

How should I store my things? Louise had been the closet and cupboard organizer. I was accustomed to putting things back in their appointed places, but I was not used to determining the logical storage spot for everything I owned. I was definitely out of my depth. Many times I mused, *Oh dear, this is unreal. Someone, please tell me it is just a dream.*

Where Louise tended to be more gregarious, outgoing and perceptive of people's needs, I used to be more introverted. Of necessity I have become more talkative, greeting strangers and making overtures of friendliness. Talking about the deaths of my wife and daughter, in order to help others with their suffering, is a more public display of personal information than I ever wanted to give. But I have discovered that tragedy has also made me more sensitive to others' hurts and needs than I had been before. I am more apt to spot the parents who lost their son to leukemia, the woman facing cancer surgery or the man whose wife left him after fifteen years of marriage.

In areas of personal weakness, such as organization, where I had relied on Louise's strengths, I had to cope alone to the best of my ability. I learned, mostly through trial and error, but it was not easy. I didn't know I shouldn't put 100 percent cotton T-shirts in the dryer on high heat. I didn't know a new red shirt being washed for the first time should be laundered by itself. Timers on electric stoves can be puzzling. How do I know the chicken is thoroughly cooked without creating a burnt offering? The real world is tough on helpless widowers!

I became aware of an idea—maybe it should be called an assumption—by friends of the griever. It is an attitude not always verbalized: "Give him a couple of months, and he will be his old self again." I believe that the vast majority of the uninitiated have no concept of the depth of hurt. Even psychiatrists once thought that the appropriate amount of time needed to recover from loss was only a few months. They now recognize that the process can take years. I confess my past ignorance and underestimation of the grieving process.

As a friend of a griever, please be aware of the time factor in the process of grief. Sensitivity in this area will make the griever's recovery a little smoother. Also, please recognize that your friend is in the process of changing to a situation that demands his facing new responsibilities and challenges. The "mix" is different without the spouse's input. Time, circumstances and the anvil of sorrow are shaping your friend into a different but, it is to be hoped, better person. The reality is that your friend is changing, so please do not assume that he will return to "his old self."

After the initial flurry of sympathy, many friends and acquaintances resume a "business-as-usual" approach. Well-wishers assume that the bereaved is "made of good stuff and will make it." That assumption may be true, but adjusting to a new life cannot be programmed like a computer. It takes time and energy, much like learning a new language. I was surprised at how extensive my wounds were and how slow the healing occurred. I had not had the occasion before to walk through the process of enormous personal grief. To say that I was unprepared is a gross understatement. Working through the grief process takes longer than a person would ever suppose.

I trust that I am more sensitive now to the sorrows of others, even a year or more after the death of a loved one. Some of the greatest encouragement and help I can give may not be in that first week following the death, but months later. Some people may be having great difficulty adjusting to a new life, or they cannot seem to let go of the old. I need to be caring but firm with fellow-grievers.

The necessity to deal with their loved one's personal things wakens many grievers to reality. Two extremes in behavior must be mentioned. One is to save everything that belonged to the deceased, even entering into a fantasy world with the loved one's things. After an extremely strong relationship, the survivor may want to relive the past, so he or she will leave everything just as it was at the time of the spouse's or child's death. I have heard of widows who have kept their husband's clothes in the closet and dresser drawers for years. His workshop is kept exactly as it was when he died. I am not sure if those widows cannot accept the death, or if they think disposing of their husband's things is an act of disloyalty bordering on treason. The Bible states, "To every thing there is a season, and a time to every purpose" (Eccles. 3:1). I do not know the season or time for sorting through possessions, but I do know that God wants me to move ahead with my life and continue to serve Him although I am now alone. I must live in the real world.

Some bereaved folk continue to cling emotionally to their loved ones for years after death. They cannot bring themselves to give that person over to God and adjust to their new life. A couple whose young son died fastened down the toys where the boy had left them at the time of his death. In the classic Dickens tale *Great Expectations* the elderly Miss Haversham, having been jilted by her fiancee, continues to wear her wedding dress as she sits in a dark cobweb-ridden room. In a similar way, some people make shrines of the deceased's room and possessions. Leaving a closet full of clothing will never bring back the wearer, nor will keeping a bedroom or workroom undisturbed somehow bring about the return of its owner.

The other extreme is getting rid of everything. Clothes, car, toys, furniture—you name it; it all goes. This behavior is less common and is more likely to occur after a relationship has soured, when the survivor wants to erase all bad memories and start a new life. Erasing every reminder of a lost loved one may be an easier choice initially; but after some time has passed, the survivor may wish for some mementos as a reminder that the person actually did exist.

I went through everything in the house during the first three months after the accident. I created three categories: keep, throw out and not sure. (In the latter category, I filed things I wanted to review later.) I gave the clothes and shoes to Louise's sisters to dispose of at their discretion. Looking at the dresses, jewelry and assorted personal effects was a jolt. I was sifting through three decades of accumulated memorabilia bearing silent witness of a wonderful life, items left by both Louise and Ruth. The experience was heart-wrenching. A plaster cast mold of a tiny hand might bring a smile of remembrance, followed closely by tears of anguish. Letters bound with a faded ribbon spoke of a precious love between my wife and me, now dreadfully separated by a split second. Looking at a dress I liked and had bought for Louise overwhelmed me.

Had my imminent return to South Africa not forced me, I might have been tempted to postpone the sorting process indefinitely. I had no choice. I had rented my house for the time I would be away and was limited for storage space. I felt greatly relieved when the sorting was over. I had confronted the memories, found them painful and been able to mourn; but when the work was done, I felt a tremendous release and a desire to carry on with my life. Looking back I can see that it was good for me to have made those decisions without delay.

The timetable for each survivor will differ. While every believer has the same Lord and is accountable to Him in sorrow, as in all matters, we each have unique situations, circumstances and personalities. May I make a few suggestions for dealing with the deceased's possessions?

Start this task without undue delay. Prioritize a list and make a flexible schedule to follow. You may wish to select a family member or friend to help you. Recognize that the process will trigger memories that are now sorrowful, but remember that in spite of the grief, we can think back on the good times and thank God for them.

Let me encourage you to keep busy in a daily routine. A regular work schedule is a good coping mechanism. Each day has its own particular tasks and problems, so get right at them. Postponing jobs can lead to daydreaming about how things used to be. If I need to prepare for a meeting, polish my shoes or wash the car, those are my first items of business. If I need to schedule a dental appointment or arrange special music for a church service, I immediately pick up the phone and make the call. Ecclesiastes 9:10 gives this advice: "Whatsoever thy hand findeth to do, do it with thy might." When I get busy doing what I should do, personal cares fade momentarily. I am not constantly thinking about them, and my mind is given a rest.

If you are the friend of a griever, encourage your friend to be active in areas other than work. Swimming, playing ball, walking and other physical exercise is good for releasing stress and tension. Playing hard definitely discourages fantasizing.

If I had been inclined to fantasize, one duty would have snapped me out of it. Dispatching official notices with death certificates to government departments and filling in insurance claims with proof of death certainly drive the cobwebs of fantasy away and make one face the clear sky of reality.

One spiritual reality that I faced head-on was the verse I frequently had used at funerals to give comfort to the bereaved. Psalm 116:15 tells us, "Precious in the sight of the LORD is the death of his saints." These words always sounded wonderful to me, but now they have a personal depth of meaning. The word "precious" is translated as "a special treasure" in Exodus 19:5 (NKJV), "honored" in Isaiah 43:4 (NKJV), and "dear" in Jeremiah 31:20. "Precious" carries the inherent concept of great value or worth. Louise's and Ruth's deaths were a horrendous tragedy and personal loss to me, but God saw it all differently. God views their deaths as the calling Home of two of His dearly loved ones. He does not measure His children's happiness in the length of time spent on this earth, but in relationship to eternity. He had Louise's and Ruth's overall well-being in mind and considered their arrival Home as a glorious moment.

When I lend something I value, I am always happy to see it safely back in my possession. I believe that the Lord has the same view when one of His children walks through the doors of Heaven;

it is a joyous occasion for Him. The Lord placed immense value in Louise's and Ruth's lives, as He does in the life of each of His children. Physical death is merely a commencement of our eternal life in Heaven. In a sense, it was a precious day for Louise and Ruth. It was their Homecoming, the day when they saw Jesus for the first time. Songwriter Carrie E. Breck penned these words:

> Face to face with Christ my Savior . . .
> Face to face—to see and know;
> Face to face with my Redeemer,
> Jesus Christ who loved me so.

While I am greatly tempted to see only my side of the situation, the reality is that I need to see God's side as well. I rejoice that the Lord counts the deaths of my loved ones as precious. If Heaven has videos cameras, I will enjoy someday replaying the expression on their faces at their Homecoming. I am cheered and comforted by the reality that Almighty God Himself regarded the arrival of Louise and Ruth in Heaven as precious. That's reality, not fantasy.

5

Feeling Exhausted

Does Jesus care when I've said good-bye
To the dearest on earth to me,
And my sad heart aches till it nearly breaks—
Is it aught to Him? does He see?

Oh yes, He cares—
I know He cares!
His heart is touched with my grief;
When the days are weary, the long nights dreary,
I know my Savior cares.

—Frank E. Graeff

The news of the accident seemed like the end of the world for me. I felt as if I had been run over by a tractor trailer loaded with forty tons of steel. Several times I cried until I could cry no more. I was completely drained. I simply had to get some sleep.

In Luke's Gospel we read that after instituting the Lord's Supper and immediately before His arrest, Jesus spent time with His disciples in the Garden of Gethsemane at the base of the Mount of

41

Olives. Jesus prayed alone three times while the disciples waited at a distance. Our Lord had instructed them to watch and pray. But Luke records that when Jesus "rose up from prayer, and was come to his disciples, he found them sleeping for sorrow" (22:45). Another translation says, "He found them asleep, exhausted from sorrow." When I read that those robust young men were so exhausted from sorrow that they fell asleep, the words leaped off the page! Sorrow of mind and heart had wiped them out. Sadness and sorrow had drained their vitality.

I now understand why the disciples couldn't stay awake. For at least a month after Louise and Ruth died, I seemed to hit a point each day where I felt my "get-up-and-go" had "got-up-and-went." Other times during the day I would snooze for anywhere from ten minutes to an hour. As the months passed, I was still having times of extreme tiredness although less than before. I began to worry that old age might be catching up with me, or that I was growing lazy. I had not known that sorrow could cause such profound exhaustion. I came to realize that this exhaustion is a normal aspect of grieving and that I do not need to feel guilty for taking an occasional nap.

Grief and exhaustion were a new combination for me. I am glad that Dr. Luke mentioned this combination in his Gospel. I do not recall having specifically been told about it before, but it makes sense. Grief is an intense emotional suffering, indicating deep, often long-term mental anguish. When I am in a state of sorrow, my body will experience times of intense tiredness. (I expect the *New England Journal of Medicine* will want a full report of my discovery!)

How am I adjusting to this exhaustion? Am I scheduling time for extra sleep, or is it "business as usual" and subsequent exhaustion? The apostle Paul wrote that we sorrow not as unbelievers who have no hope, but we *do* sorrow. I must take exhaustion into account and adjust my lifestyle accordingly, or I am headed for trouble. If I don't get enough rest, I could fall asleep while driving or praying or listening to a message. Exhaustion could cause me to become impatient, short-tempered and more forgetful than usual. Scheduling rest time is not something grown men and women in the West usually do, except on a Sunday afternoon. Planning extra sleeping time was certainly not easy for me, because I found that in addition to the tasks I was accustomed to performing, I also needed to take on the jobs that Louise had always done. That meant I had extra work and had to take decisive action to provide time for the needed naps. One solution was that I gave low-priority tasks an even lower priority or eliminated them altogether.

In trying to help those who are grieving, we need to be aware that they may be weighed down with extra responsibilities and "exhausted from sorrow." Maybe my fellow church members or I could provide needed assistance for a sorrowing soldier so that he or she does not burn out. Cleaning the house, washing the car, cooking meals or doing the laundry are just some of the practical ways to "bear ye one another's burdens," as the apostle Paul suggested in Galatians 6:2.

Just as we do, Jesus experienced tiredness. In John 4:6 we read that He was "weary from his journey." In three of the Gospels we read that on a certain occasion He was asleep in a boat when a violent storm arose and the disciples thought they would all drown. The disciples were terrorized by fear. In desperation they awoke the sleeping Jesus, who merely spoke and the wind and the waves immediately subsided. How could Jesus have been asleep in the midst of a terrific storm? I suggest that He was extremely tired—so much so that the howling wind and raging sea did not awaken Him. Grieving, stress and emotional upheaval exhaust a person. He has to sleep. Sleep seizes him, and he is unable to do anything except succumb to its irresistible power.

Our Lord knows all about this emotional upheaval and exhaustion. Even though Jesus is God of very God, He came to this earth as a human being. He was born in a barn and reared in poverty by our standards. While He lived on this earth, He experienced both joys and trials. He undoubtedly saw sibling rivalry. Perhaps His grandparents died. He probably ran, fell and scraped His knees. We read that He hungered, thirsted and became tired. He felt the love and devotion of followers such as John and Mary Magdalene. He felt the sting of betrayal by Judas Iscariot. Adoring crowds hung on every word He spoke. Yet certain Jewish religious leaders and crowds screamed in frenzied hatred, "Crucify Him!" He felt the anguish of nails being driven into His hands and feet. He died an agonizing death. He knows what we go through.

The Holy Spirit prompted the writer of Hebrews to write, "For we have not an high priest which cannot be touched with the feeling of our infirmities; but was in all points tempted like as we are, yet without sin. Let us therefore come boldly unto the throne of grace, that we may obtain mercy, and find grace to help in time of need" (Heb. 4:15,16).

I knew that I was able to go to God through prayer in Jesus' name with complete confidence in the One who would sympathize with me. I had the promise that I could "obtain mercy and find grace to help" in any time of need. And what better time than now? I did go to Him for help. In fact, I went to Him so often that I even began to wonder if God would get tired of my telling Him about my broken heart.

God gives good news to people in every difficult situation. In Psalm 147:3 He says, "He healeth the broken in heart, and bindeth up their wounds." The word "wounds" literally means "sorrows." We have the assurance that He will give comfort and rest to those who are "exhausted from sorrow." We find this wonderful promise in Matthew 11:28: "Come unto me, all ye that labour and are heavy laden, and I will give you rest."

6

Dealing with Guilt and Anger

While they have gained, we losers are,
We miss them day by day;
But thou canst every breach repair,
And wipe our tears away.
We pray, as in Elisha's case,
When great Elijah went
May double portions of thy grace,
To us who stay, be sent.

—Isaac Newton

I n experiencing grief, guilt feelings may often arise. Guilt has been defined as the gnawing voice of conscience. I spent hours sitting or lying on my bed thinking, *If only I had been home, Louise, Ruth and I would have traveled together and left at a different time.* Or, *If I had not been visiting churches, things would be different today.* Or, *If I had weeded the garden more often, Louise would have been more pleased with me.* Similar thoughts crossed my mind continuously, as I am sure have crossed other grievers' minds. I have no doubt that Satan, "the accuser of the brethren," enjoyed fanning the flames of guilt during my time of great vulnerability.

Some survivors look for evidence of their failure toward the deceased. The bereaved accuse themselves of negligence, exaggerating minor omissions and commissions. I could destroy myself by racking my brain with questions such as these: Did I ever speak too harshly to Ruthie? Did I ever unjustly accuse her of disobedience? Or, Did I really love Louise as Christ loves the Church? Did I criticize her dress? Was I ever unkind in my remarks about her cooking? Did I ever overlook her sacrifice on my behalf? Did I complain about chores that needed to be done?

When I hear a man complaining that his wife wants him to pick up the dry cleaning on the way home from work, I feel a little envious. I would be willing to take out the garbage, wash and wax the car by hand, mow the lawn, trim the hedges, repair the leaking faucets and any other dreaded chore if only it would bring Louise and Ruth back.

One day as I was sitting around a dining room table with a young couple, the wife asked her husband if he had completed one of those "Honey do . . ." jobs. He hadn't got around to it yet. Quick as a flash she said, "You'll feel sorry if I die." I could see a gigantic load of guilt landing on the husband's back. Looking the wife squarely in the eyes, I said softly yet firmly, "Don't you ever, ever say that again." Legitimate guilt is one thing; guilt trips that one person lays on another are something else. Guilt is a common experience regarding the death of a spouse. "If I had only taken her to another doctor and hospital, she might be living today." Perhaps more could have been done, but using guilt as a motivator is destructive.

Guilt feelings are a normal part of the acceptance process and should be recognized and dealt with for what they are. I had to realize that I was not responsible for Louise's and Ruth's deaths. Even had I been a perfect husband and father, I could not have prevented the accident.

When an unexpected death occurs, the opportunity to say, "I was wrong. I'm sorry. Please forgive me" is lost. Then the feeling of guilt over unsettled issues becomes more intense. When Louise and Ruth died, what could I do about my unresolved sins toward them? Resolution was possible only through application of Scriptural truth. God's forgiveness is the only means of wiping the slate clean and receiving release from guilt feelings. "If we confess our sins, he is faithful and just to forgive us our sins, and to cleanse us from all unrighteousness" (1 John 1:9).

My responsibility is to acknowledge and sincerely confess my sins to God through Jesus Christ. He will forgive me. I can now "think forgiven" and "live forgiven." When God forgives, He forgives forever. I then change my sinful behavior and replace it with Biblical practices. I could be guilt-ridden over something I did or said to Louise or Ruth, but I choose to rejoice in God's provision of forgiveness and restoration to the "joy of my salvation." The psalmist described the joy and peace of forgiveness in Psalm 32:1 and 2a: "Blessed is he whose transgression is forgiven, whose sin is covered. Blessed is the man unto whom the LORD imputeth not iniquity. . . ."

One area I feel some guilt about is taking things for granted. I now have made a resolution: "I will never take anything for granted again." I know that I will fail to keep that resolution fully, but I am more aware than ever before of the transience of life. I assumed that Louise would outlive me. She was two years younger than I, and I know that men, on the average, die five years earlier than women. So I thought I would be the first to die. I took it for granted that we would see our golden wedding anniversary. I would enjoy Louise's raisin bran muffins forever. She would take care of me. And Ruth, my talkative daughter, would be around to the end of my earthly road, when she would say with love and tears, "See you later, Daddy." In my wildest dreams I never imagined anything else.

Am I going to take things for granted again? Not on your life! I relish—even by myself—a beautiful sunset, ducks swimming in a pond, a stroll around the block, flowers blooming in the park, the sound of a woman's voice, a home-cooked meal. I will never again ignore these simple pleasures. Being human, and particularly a man, I may become careless, but I will work hard at relishing the joys and blessings of life more than I ever did before. I am taking time now to "smell the roses" and enjoy the simple amenities life affords every day.

Guilt feelings often erupt in anger. I could become angry with myself because I think that perhaps I am to blame for the loss. I could become angry with anyone and everyone I assign with responsibility for causing death or loss. I could even become angry with God for not preventing it. I felt the waves of anger lapping on the beach of my mind, but God enabled me to keep anger from controlling me. I have always maintained that life's trials make one either a bitter or better person, and I am consciously striving for the latter.

Actually, anger was not much of a problem for me. I am not the type of person who normally becomes angry. Besides, after the accident I was aching in grief so much that I didn't entertain angry thoughts. The biggest credit for controlling my anger, however, belongs to the Lord. He gave me grace day by day to respond positively to Biblical principles.

My sorrow did not express itself against the driver of the car that crossed the median, striking our car. For many people revenge is a primary and consuming thought. The Bible states that revenge is wrong. If there is any "paying back" to be done, it is not for me to do. "Vengeance is mine; I will repay," says the Lord. My paraphrase of these words from Romans 12:19 is, "Do not take revenge; that is God's jurisdiction." When vengeful thoughts came to me, I never entertained revenge as an option. The other driver was asleep and did not suffer major injuries. No matter how he was driving, whether awake or asleep, driving recklessly or not, my anger or revenge at him would not bring back my wife and daughter. The thought that kept recurring to me was this: Louise and Ruth will never be back. Whether the other driver is fined one dollar or ten thousand dollars or if he is jailed for one day or for ten years is immaterial. The results are the same for me—I'll never see Louise or Ruth again in this life. I can honestly say that I have no desire for revenge.

As your grieving friend experiences guilt, seek to counterbalance any excessive self-blame. Certainly no one is perfect, and words and deeds that should not have been committed or actions that were neglected will rise like specters to haunt the survivor. Remind your friend of God's promises to forgive the truly penitent, and encourage him to read Psalm 32. If his extreme sense of guilt persists, direct your friend to a carefully chosen professional for counseling.

While the griever strikes out in anger at whomever he may feel is responsible for the death of his loved one, your calm presence and reasoning influence may enable your friend to constructively express his strong emotions. Continually reassure your friend of your unconditional love.

7

Working through the Pain of Loss

Christ mourned at tomb of Lazarus
    He realized the loss—
The darkness of "the valley,"
    The shadows of the cross,
The bitter grief at parting,
    The pain that mothers feel;
He wept, though he was ready
    The human grief to heal.

Oh, there are tears for dying,
    And heartbreak by the grave;
There's a loneliness and sighing;
    But Christians should be brave.
For one who passed before us
    Came back that we might see
That soul-life is eternal.
    Let this your comfort be.
          —Dorothy Dix Porges

Sometimes I desperately want Louise and Ruth back. In my mind, I relive precious moments we had together: a chicken dinner at the Swiss Chalet, an evening at the Toronto Skydome or praying together over some problem. I have to force myself to accept the enormity of my personal loss, which threatens to overwhelm me. At such times I am like the needle on a gauge that is "off the charts." My mind simply cannot accept such an incredible overload. I have hit my head on the corner of a cupboard door, have severely sprained my ankle and have had five gall bladder attacks. They caused pain, but they were nothing in comparison to the pain of losing Louise and Ruth.

Have you ever lost a valuable, highly treasured ring or large sum of money? Have you had a house fire that destroyed irreplaceable photos and heirlooms? Even time lost is a missed opportunity that can never be recaptured. All of these incidents produce feelings of loss. An emptiness settles into the depths of one's being.

You know you have lost something that can never be replaced or substituted. Rings, photo albums, money or heirlooms are like a ten-dollar bill to a millionaire. Such things are "peanuts" compared to the "millions" that I have lost. What is the value of a loving wife? Proverbs 31:10 states, "Her price [worth] is far above rubies."

I have lost my constant companion of thirty-three years: my best friend, lover, confidant, back massager, the mother of my children and the woman with whom I planned to spend yet another thirty-three years. Louise was all this and more to me. I still turn to share some small comment or insight with her, and I hurt afresh when I remember that she is not here and never again will be. It's like losing her all over again, and I fight the tears.

My dear Ruthie was a special delight to me, perhaps because she was my only daughter. I miss her confidences and chats about daily life. Ruth could make the most routine event sound exciting. Sometimes when I'm lost in thought and the phone rings, I think, *Oh, it's Ruth wanting to tell me about her day at school.* But, of course, it isn't. One aspect of Ruth's death especially pained me—her age; she was only twenty-nine. Her being so young made the pain of loss even greater.

Louise and Ruth are with their Savior in Heaven, but I miss their companionship. I miss the give-and-take of human relationships, the day-in, day-out routine of life. I have no one to contradict or congratulate me, no one to correct me, no one to sit quietly with. I even miss Louise saying, "Did you . . . ?" which she usually asked when I did not have the job done.

In the first three or four months, the loss is the first thing you think about when you wake up in the morning and the last before you go to bed at night. It occupies every waking hour. Ever so slowly you find yourself "forgetting" to think about your loss. The forgetting process is not like a straight line on a graph, but a jagged line, indicating the ups and downs in the process of healing the pain of loss. In time you find yourself not thinking of your loved one quite as much, since new experiences and relationships develop in your life; but the pangs of pain and loss are like a sore thumb that can be hit at any moment, bringing instant pain.

Knowing that things will never be the way they used to be—that my beloved wife and daughter will not drive to the house—at first made me want to just walk and walk or to lose consciousness in sleep because the loss was intolerable. The pain of loss was like the ache of an abscessed tooth—throbbing and anguishing. I found that almost anything aggravated the pain: seeing old photos or memorabilia, places, people, special days, favorite foods and restaurants, an empty house, a house full of guests, eating alone, eating with a group, socializing with couples. So much reminds me of my loss. The wound takes a long time to heal because something always reopens it.

The pain of loss is long-term; it has no instant cure. There are no magic wands. Like the common cold, it must work itself out of one's system at its own speed.

The pain cannot be avoided by overwork. I was tempted to bury myself in my work, but frantic activity does not take away the pain.

The pain should not be exaggerated through wallowing in self-pity. It is tempting to reason, "Look at me, I've lost my wife and daughter. My son lives thousands of miles away. I'm all alone. Added to this I spend my life in a foreign country away from my church and friends. Woe is me."

The pain cannot be cured by using drugs or alcohol. These merely mask it for a brief time.

Experiencing the pain of loss can be compared to a person with a fear of heights (a medical condition known as acrophobia) who unwittingly gets on a super-duper roller coaster and has no alternative but to ride it out.

It was good for me to acknowledge both privately and publicly that my loved ones have gone Home to their Father. I do not want to deny reality or try to deceive myself. I need to state that Louise and Ruth are His, and if He wants them Home with Himself, I release my claims to them. I must let them go and thank my Father for the privilege I had to share their lives with them. No one can ever take away the memories.

The years with Louise were wonderful. God gave us two children, whom we trained to love and serve Him. For a while we had a snowmobile and a small boat for fishing, which we all loved to use. We traveled to England, Israel and Guatemala. We planted two churches in Ontario. We spent part of our two years with ABWE in South Africa, evangelizing in that needy country after spending twenty-nine years of pastoring in Canada. We endured the health threat of Louise's breast cancer.

Ruthie was with me from the beginning to the end of her earthly life. During kindergarten, she announced that she was going to be a teacher. She never wavered from that decision. She had a natural gift for teaching, as did her mother. Ruth loved music. She took piano and voice lessons for many years, using her skills in church and school. No father could have wanted a more loyal daughter. The pain of loss is greater because she was such a wonderful daughter.

God heals the pain of loss through the Scriptures. I read and reread the psalms. They were like cool water to a thirsty man. The passages deal with emotions that I could readily identify with: death, forsakenness, betrayal, fear, hurt. As the writers poured out their hearts to God, I could readily relate to such phrases as, "Why art thou cast down, O my soul? And why art thou disquieted in me?" (Ps. 42:5) I found in the Scriptures encouragement and peace. "The righteous cry, and the LORD heareth, and delivereth them out of all their troubles. The LORD is nigh unto those that are of a broken heart; and saveth such as be of a contrite spirit" (Ps. 34:17, 18).

God heals the pain of loss through prayer. Hundreds of people prayed earnestly for me. James 5:16 tells us, "The effectual fervent prayer of a righteous man availeth much." I sincerely believe God heard those prayers and ministered healing to me.

If we will allow God to work in our lives, trials and pain (both emotional and physical) can drive us to a deeper relationship with the Lord. In lonely, painful hours I sought the Lord and found Him always available to give me strength to trust Him with my pain. He heard when I cried out in prayer, and I knew He understood as He had understood Mary and Martha when they mourned for their brother, Lazarus.

He used not only the prayers but also the fellowship of the people of God to heal me. We prayed, sang, cried, laughed, played and joked together. Someone would telephone or visit; an encouraging letter would arrive—the very tonic needed at the moment.

Many situations in life boggle our minds; we wonder how we will ever get through them. In college I was constantly amazed when the professors handed out syllabi at the beginning of the semester. I would look at the lists of required essays and term papers, wondering in panic how I could possibly complete the assignments on time. I knew I would never be able to handle the mountain of work. But I did, one page at a time.

In my severe trial I complained, "I can't handle this." God replied, "My grace is sufficient for thee: for my strength is made perfect in weakness." I was greatly helped by studying and meditating on the verses in 2 Corinthians 12:7–9. Paul experienced a "thorn in the flesh" (v. 7) that God allowed Satan to buffet him with, lest Paul's vision of Paradise would make him too proud. The buffeting was severe. Three times Paul pled with the Lord to remove the affliction. The answer of our all-wise God was, "My grace is sufficient for thee." Paul was not going to be miraculously relieved of the trial, but he would experience God's power in his life, enabling him to live victoriously with the affliction. Paul's, mine or your "thorn in the flesh" is no match for the grace of God.

The Lord said, "For my strength is made perfect in weakness." Our extremity is God's opportunity. God is more than able to walk us through the pain of loss. His power will be shown in our lives so that we and others will recognize that triumph comes not on our own, but through the power of Christ working in us. Christ wants to use my feeble life, and I need to get self-pity and pride out of His way so He can do the job He desires. We can give a testimony to outsiders as they see us swept along by the strengthening grace of God.

What was Paul's reaction to God's promise? "Most gladly therefore will I rather glory in my infirmities, that the power of Christ may rest upon me. Therefore I take pleasure in infirmities, in reproaches, in necessities, in persecutions, in distresses for Christ's sake: for when I am weak, then am I strong" (2 Cor. 12:9, 10). God does not give us grace just to endure pain, grief and affliction; He wants His power to "rest upon me," to transform my liability into an asset for His glory. My weakness becomes a strength in God's hands. Some may think that if God loves us, we will not experience any pain. This idea is not true; Paul hurt, I hurt. The difference is that God's grace gives us the power to handle the pain in a manner honoring to God.

As we walk through pain and grief or live with a "thorn," we have available to us the power of Christ to overcome. The pain exists, but Christian character is built. God is both helping and molding me. Some have remarked to me, "I don't know how you handle it!" I can't, but God can. For His sake I accept grief so that the power of Christ may rest upon me.

You may not be able to empathize with the pain and loss your friend is experiencing. Like the process of giving birth, where the father can't go through labor for the mother, only the griever can work through the feelings of the pain of loss. Do not minimize his experience by saying something inane like, "I know what you are going through. I once lost a cat." That's like telling someone with an inoperable brain tumor that you once had a hangnail. So what? How can that begin to compare with the enormity of the present situation? Instead, let your friend know that you are praying for him and are available to help.

A prosperous lawyer, esteemed in his profession, Horatio Spafford saw the loss of his business in the great Chicago fire of 1871. He turned his home in the suburbs into a haven for many homeless victims of the fire. But trials were far from over for that man of God. Mrs. Spafford, in giving herself without stint to help the needy and homeless, became exhausted; and the family doctor suggested that a sea voyage would help her regain her strength. So passage was booked for her and their four daughters. Spafford planned to join them later. But the *Ville du Havre* was not to arrive in its French port. On a starry night, on a quiet sea, the luxury liner was rammed by an iron sailing vessel. Despite the heroic efforts of the seamen and the help of a rescue ship, all four of the Spaffords' little girls were drowned. Mrs. Spafford's cable nine days later, from Cardiff, Wales, read, "Saved alone." Mr. Spafford searched his life for some explanation. The Chicago fire, the loss of his business— now this stunning quadruple loss. Night after night he paced the floor, till one morning he turned to a friend and said, "I am glad to trust my Lord when it will cost me something." Following this tragedy he wrote the triumphant hymn that has blessed generations of God's people:

> When peace, like a river, attendeth my way,
> When sorrows like sea billows roll—
> Whatever my lot, Thou hast taught me to say,
> It is well, it is well with my soul.

8

Asking Why

My life is but a weaving
*   Between my Lord and me,*
I cannot choose the colors
*   He worketh steadily.*

Ofttimes He weaveth sorrow.
*   And I in foolish pride*
Forget He sees the upper
*   And I the underside.*

Not till the loom is silent
*   And the shuttles cease to fly*
Shall God unroll the canvas
*   And explain the reason why.*

The dark threads are as needful
*   In the weaver's skillful hand*
As the threads of gold and silver
*   In the pattern He has planned.*
*   —Grant Colfax Tullar*

Why, Lord, why? I have asked the Lord this question countless times. My mind says that there must be a rational explanation why God would allow Louise and Ruth to be taken from me, but nothing seems to make sense. Why would two talented and dedicated Christians be snatched away by death? Why not allow mass murderers to experience a fatal car accident instead? Why not permit drug dealers to lose their lives? I was tempted to lash out at the unfairness of it all.

Asking why is one of the steps in the grief process. In the early days of my grief, it was a recurring theme. This constant recurring was frustrating, because I never came up with an answer to the burning question gnawing at the center of my being. If Louise had been eighty-six and riddled with cancer, the question would not have arisen. We ask why when events are not what we expect.

When I asked why, it seemed as if there were no answers. Slowly, however, I realized that the infinite Creator of the universe cannot be comprehended by human creatures like me, bound by parameters of time and space. To my mind came the words of the prophet Isaiah: "For my thoughts are not your thoughts, neither are your ways my ways, saith the LORD. For as the heavens are higher than the earth, so are my ways higher than your ways, and my thoughts than your thoughts" (Isa. 55:8, 9).

God's thoughts and actions are beyond my comprehension. His understanding is without limitation; mine is limited. My understanding is warped by prejudice, ignorance and the influence of the culture in which I live. God is entirely perfect in every way. No wonder I have a problem understanding His plans. I am learning to accept what I cannot change and looking forward to the day when His reasons will be revealed. Then I will fall down in worship and praise.

Not just in crushing, traumatic situations, but even in everyday life we find ourselves asking why. I remember when Louise was looking for a teaching position in an elementary school just before we were married. I was taking a full load at college and could work only part-time, so a job for Louise was absolutely necessary. She was an A student with good references from her student teaching, and teaching positions were available. We knew she would be hired immediately. Wrong! To her dumbfounded disbelief, her application was turned down. *Why Lord? We're preparing to serve You. Why this obstacle?* The following week we shared our disappointment with some Christian friends who "just happened" to know of a school that was still looking for teachers. Those friends made some phone calls, and the very next day Louise had a position with better pay in a brand-new school. That experience was the first of many occasions as a couple, and later as a family, when God did not do what we thought He should, but later we could see His benevolent wisdom in directing our lives.

It would be wonderful to give our unsolvable problems to God all the time and then just leave them with Him. Unfortunately we have a tendency to continue to worry over them, never solving the questions but giving ourselves big headaches. Because God has revealed Himself as loving, just and compassionate in ways I cannot begin to fathom, and because He is capable beyond my wildest imagining, I can be sure that He does what is best. Life holds no surprises, no "glitches," no "OOPS!" for God. He did not need a telephone call to learn that Louise and Ruth Stephenson had had a fatal car accident that Saturday in May 1993. Nor did He require notification that Wally and David Stephenson were sorely in need of comfort. God knew the details before the events ever occurred. He allowed the accident to happen. Actually, it was not an "accident"; it was an incident completely known to God.

I had never been tested with whys to that degree before, but when I turned from questioning to worshiping my all-wise Father, a sense of hope and tranquillity returned to my life. I am a rational type; and slowly, in the days following the accident, the rational side gained the upper hand over the emotional side. Had I allowed myself to wallow in "Why me?" and "I deserve better treatment than I am getting," my attitude would have rendered me useless to God. While I am not obligated to enjoy everything that God does, I am required to obey Him. I am working hard to replace my questions with confidence in God's sovereign plan. By faith, I am trying to accept God's will, and I am learning to be at peace. Philippians 4:6 and 7 tell us, "Be anxious for nothing, but in everything by prayer and supplication, with thanksgiving, let your requests be made known to God; and the peace of God, which surpasses all understanding, will guard your hearts and minds through Christ Jesus" (NKJV).

One of the best-loved American poets of the nineteenth century, John Greenleaf Whittier (1807–1892), wrote of God's goodness amid trials:

> I see the wrong that round me lies,
> I feel the guilt within,
> I hear, with groan and travail cries,
> The world confess its sin.
> Yet, in the maddening maze of things,
> And tossed by storm and flood,
> To one fixed trust my spirit clings:
> I know that God is good!

My friends were wise in encouraging me to turn my whys over to God. Trying to figure out all the whys and wherefores of life's mysteries is like a dog chasing its tail—there is no end to the circle of questions. We all want answers. Sometimes we simply must acknowledge there are no satisfactory answers. Someone has said,

"Don't put a question mark where God has put a period." I am trying to accept my friends' advice to give my whys to God. Counsel your grieving friend to do likewise.

After a slow, agonizing search for plausible reasons, defeated, I have concluded that in this life I will never know the reason why. But I am convinced that some day in Heaven it will all be made clear to me. Then I will stand, worshiping in awe of God's wisdom and goodness.

9

Cherishing Memories

God is! Christ loves! Christ lives!
And by his own returning gives
Sure proofs of immortality,
The firstfruits he: and we
The harvest of his victory.
The life beyond shall this life far transcend,
And death is the beginning not the end.

—*Author Unknown*

From the moment I heard of the deaths of my beloved family members, memories flooded over me like wave after wave crashing on a beach. I had known an enormous bond of respect and love with both my wife and my daughter. We had many fabulous experiences together. At Christmas Louise and Ruth went all out with food, gifts and decorations. They baked cookies and cakes for weeks ahead of time. Our house was filled with the aroma of fruitcake, shortbread and other holiday goodies. My favorite was called the New York Square: two thick layers of chocolate with a luscious cream filling. Louise always brought me one fresh from the pan as soon as it was done. Ropes of evergreen festooned our window ledges; and pots of red, white and pink poinsettias sat prominently throughout the house. Wreaths of pine cones, holly and vines as well as silk flower arrangements and centerpieces graced the house. Louise was artistically talented. Even the bathrooms were tastefully decorated with holiday towels and scented pine candle arrangements. With memories like that, I didn't have the heart to do anything for Christmas 1993. I didn't get a tree for my house in Cape Town, put up decorations or buy any gifts. I sent my son David a check, and he sent me a watch that didn't arrive until January. Christmas had too many memories to celebrate alone.

I can vividly recall other memories: Blue Jays games as we shouted ourselves hoarse cheering on our favorite baseball team. At a few games our shouts turned to dismay.

I remember quiet evenings at home with Louise in her well-worn burgundy bathrobe and fuzzy slippers, sipping black coffee as she discussed the children in her kindergarten class.

I remember one time when Louise sent thank-you notes to our financial donors. After her signature, as was her custom, she added a Scripture reference. She meant to write 1 Samuel 12:24, which speaks of the wonderful things God does for us. Instead, she wrote 2 Samuel 12:24, which reads, "Then David comforted Bathsheba his wife, and went in unto her, and lay with her." When we discovered the error, we howled with laughter and hoped none of the donors actually looked up the reference.

One year we celebrated Christmas in Florida. It was so cold that we walked around Disney World in our parkas. Once we went camping near Banff, Alberta. Louise surprised a bear behind our tent trailer, or was it the bear that surprised Louise? Then there was the time we visited relatives at Walnut Creek and San Juan Bautista, California, and David's brand-new special kite crashed into a very tall tree. We had to call the park ranger to retrieve it.

Birthdays, vacations, conferences—the list goes on and on. These memories are now tinged with sorrow; but because I have these recollections, Louise and Ruth will always be with me. As long as memory lasts, my wife and daughter will live in those frozen moments of time, yelling at a baseball game, viewing Niagara Falls or just pushing a shopping cart through the supermarket. The pain of recall lessens with time, although I doubt that it will ever vanish completely.

As time goes on, however, the character of the memories changes. I have noticed that widows particularly have difficulty accurately portraying their husbands. They recall only virtues and happy times, and they almost idolize their partners. With all due respect to Louise and Ruth, who were among the finest of wives and daughters, like all of us they were not worthy of deification. I trust that my recollections will portray a sensitive, balanced perspective of them to myself and others.

To those who are sorrowing or comforting those in sorrow, may I suggest that you talk about your loved ones and recall the times together. I don't avoid sharing my memories; but even as I talk and laugh about some of the old times, I feel a twinge in my heart.

While I treasure memories of my old life, I am consciously building a repertoire of new memories. I find that I am slowly able to include happenings that do not involve my wife or daughter, memories of events that have taken place since their sudden deaths and therefore hold no sadness: memories in Cape Town of Everglen Baptist Church member Allan Joy barbecuing mountains of chicken, lamb, pork chops, steaks and *boerewors* (farmer's sausage) for the entire church family and of Steve du Toit chasing his two German shepherds out of the house. Memories from the West Coast of British Columbia where I visited David's little bachelor apartment, toured Butchart Gardens and had tea at the Empress Hotel.

Recalling cherished memories has been a severe trial for me. In James 1:2–4 we read, "My brethren, count it all joy when ye fall into [various trials]; knowing this, that the trying of your faith worketh patience. But let patience have her perfect work, that ye may be perfect and entire, wanting nothing." Remembering has brought bittersweet joy, but I feel that reliving memories is helping to produce in me the qualities of patience, endurance and perseverance. Just as the heat of the flame burns imperfection from gold to produce a pure product, in the same way through trials, I am becoming a more sensitive, caring and helpful person. More than ever before, I now sense the loneliness of the widowed, the pain of the griever and the hopelessness caused by the abject poverty suffered by millions of South Africans. I rejoice in my spiritual growth thus far and trust that I will not resist trials that could profit me, just to avoid pain and suffering.

The Bible echoes with calls to remembrance. Deuteronomy

32:7 tells us to "remember the days of old, consider the years of many generations." The Lord told Isaiah to "remember the former things of old" (Isa. 46:9). In trying to help your friend who is going through grief, be sure he realizes that he has thousands of memories that he should cherish as a gift from God. Encourage him to savor the good memories and thank God for them. For example, today is Saturday. When our kids were young, our favorite Saturday breakfast included generous helpings of blueberry pancakes smothered with real maple syrup. *Lord, thank You for such memories.*

Before a lump of clay becomes a Royal Doulton figurine, it must go through multiple moldings, firings and glazings. But the end product is beautiful and well worth the effort involved to create it. God seeks to make His human lumps of clay into people who glorify Him. The memories I crave to possess twenty years down the road of life are these: I became a better person, and I had a strong positive impact on others who were grieving. May other people remember me as one who profited spiritually from trials and turned stumbling blocks into stepping-stones.

10

Adjusting to Life

His grace is sufficient, whate'er may befall,
Perhaps, even now, you may hear His sweet call;
"Come, cast upon me all thy conflicts and care;
I'll carry thy burdens, thy sorrows I'll share;
In faithfulness I all thy comfort shall be,
I'll give consolation, O, come unto me."

—Selected

One of my first thoughts after receiving Alex's call that Saturday in May 1993 was that my life was in for massive change. The emotional upheaval was one aspect, but the physical and social void was another.

During the first few weeks following the accident, I could deal with only the funeral and other immediate details. I had to send hundreds of "thank you" cards acknowledging donations to charities. My sister Marion was a great help with that task. My brother Al and his wife, Gail, did whatever they could for me. They win the Nobel prize for practical help in a family crisis.

Initially I did not make plans for the future beyond the previously made arrangements to return to South Africa. One day at a time was all I could handle, all I asked the Lord for. I knew that

His strength and grace were sufficient for each day and that if I got through the rough times, one day things would "come right," as the South Africans say.

I had to learn to sleep again. I had always been a good sleeper. I could sleep through a violent thunderstorm or the cries of Ruth and David as babies. After the accident my sleep was broken every night. I was as restless as a bear in a zoo; constantly moving, fidgeting and going to the bathroom. I found myself wide awake at 3:00 A.M., wandering aimlessly around the house. It took almost two years to get my sleeping pattern back.

Then the cooking! Both Louise and Ruth could cook a meal that would make Queen Elizabeth II drool. Louise was known as "the muffin lady." As I write this, I am salivating and crying. My taste buds crave Louise's cherry cheesecake and a thick slice of juicy prime rib. My cooking skills are elementary, rudimentary—even those may be generous descriptions. Can you imagine the state of self-pity I entered at the thought of facing my own cooking for the rest of my life?

My problems with cooking started at the supermarket. How much should I buy for one person? Louise and I regularly invited guests for lunch and dinner, so we usually bought in large quantities. I was too uncomfortable, however, to foist on friends and strangers my own cooking, a term I use loosely. Since my small experience was in buying food in a large quantity, I purchased too much and had to throw things out. I had to train myself to buy just one chicken breast, a small steak, one apple or tomato or just two Kaiser rolls. I had a hard time learning to buy only what I could eat within a few days so the food would not spoil. I ate bananas three days in a row, then I had to eat the grapes before they rotted. I ate spaghetti for a week. I never did eat a whole head of lettuce before it began to wilt.

I discovered that the best system for me was to shop three times a week. At first I felt a little self-conscious at the checkout when the clerk rang up a small amount of sliced roast beef or twenty-five cents' worth of tomatoes. The staff soon recognized me as a regular, if not eccentric, customer.

But when I had the food in my kitchen, what would I do with it? The prospect of cooking for myself and eating alone was psychologically overwhelming. Louise was the cook in our house, and

I had practically no notion of how to fend for myself in the kitchen. When she died, I had little interest in eating, let alone learning culinary skills. In my first ten months alone, I averaged cooking two meals each month. I ate a lot of fruit; sliced roast beef, which I bought at the supermarket; whole wheat bread; raisin bran flakes and some hard-boiled eggs. If it had not been for the friends at Everglen Church in Cape Town and Southlands Church in Durban who brought in meals regularly, I might well have starved. I must admit that I never discouraged anyone from inviting the missionary pastor over for dinner!

Eating by myself was another hurdle. Louise and I used to chat during meals. We discussed the day's events, our upcoming schedules, our children and anything else that interested us. When I eat alone, I miss the conversation and companionship of another person in general, and of Louise in particular. Eating alone has none of the camaraderie and sparkle of dining with even one other person. For someone like me who views eating as a social event, eating alone is a lackluster, mechanical activity. I detest eating in restaurants by myself, and I dislike fast-food takeout. If I have to eat alone, I'll just make a sandwich at home. To avoid that situation, I look for ways to eat meals in company, or I make plans with friends to "brown bag" together, dine at a restaurant or have a picnic.

Since I can't arrange company all the time, I work on planning, cooking and eating the meals that I must eat alone. I set the table and include a flower in a vase or a candle. I sit down to the strains of instrumental music and slowly savor every morsel of the meal. I don't do this every day, of course, but I do make the effort occasionally. I might as well make mealtime as palatable as possible.

Socializing has greatly helped me to adjust to my new reality. I have found that I need to take the initiative and telephone one or two friends to ask if we can get together. Our entertainment is simple and unsophisticated: a meal together, a game of Uno and a Coke or just sitting around solving the world's problems. What good times we have! I enjoy myself as we eat, talk, laugh and play together.

Church friends have accused me of being helpless and hopeless at housekeeping. Not exactly encouraging words. I never claimed to be Molly the Maid, skilled in keeping house. I just try to get by with the bare essentials. Why should I make my bed in the morning when I have to pull the covers down again at night to get into bed? If I leave the bed unmade, it is all ready. By many standards, I am getting failing grades in domestic arts. Louise never faulted my dish washing and vacuuming, which were my strengths, but I've been forced to add to my repertoire of domestic chores.

In the area of washing clothes, I am learning the hard way. The washer works fine as long as I remember to empty my shirts' and pants' pockets before I start the machine. One week I left a ballpoint pen in a dress-shirt pocket. Someone ought to invent washing machines that come equipped with scanners to prevent such occurrences.

Driving is another hard adjustment. Louise was my navigator and chief defensive coordinator. No, she wasn't a backseat driver, but if I were unfamiliar with an address, she would tell me the streets coming up, warn me of an oncoming car or road condition she thought I may not have noticed, and give other helpful suggestions. Now I have to pay attention to all this myself.

More important than these things, I miss a human touch, a kiss and a hug. A pillow doesn't provide much tactile response. A door jam doesn't give quite the same massage that soothing fingers do. Gaining experience in the learning-to-live-again category has no adequate substitute for what I so often took for granted. To the married person reading this I say, "Go and give your spouse a big kiss."

We used to enjoy driving along country roads, swimming at a Cape Town area beach called The Strand, or leisurely dining at a steakhouse. In the seven months of glorious summer weather after I returned to South Africa, I did not attempt to do any of those activities by myself. I did not want to do them alone, although I had enjoyed doing them with Louise. Since my life has changed, I am struggling to find new ways of spending my leisure hours. I read a book or watch an educational program or a sports event on TV or telephone a few friends. One activity I greatly enjoy is walking. I find watching nature and cars and people relaxing. If the weather is bad, I go to a mall and walk around smartly several times.

I am learning to give all of my cares to my Heavenly Father. That does not mean that I never plan ahead or think about these issues; but I try not to fume, fuss or lose sleep over them. My Father knows me and my needs, so why should I worry? I don't just sit and do nothing; I do what I am able to and trust God with what I am unable to do. I ask God to answer my requests as He sees fit.

Over the years I have tried personally and have encouraged others to cast their burdens and anxieties on the Lord. "Cast thy burden upon the LORD, and he shall sustain thee" (Ps. 55:22). "Casting all your care upon him; for he careth for you" (1 Pet. 5:7). In adjusting to my new life I have had plenty of opportunity to practice casting my cares on the Lord.

When I go to my bank and deposit money into my savings account, I never lose a moment's sleep wondering whether the bank will fail or if I will ever see my money, plus accrued interest, again. Am I foolish? Should I go to the bank daily to get a statement of my investment or ask to see my money? No. I leave the money with the bank and never give it another thought. My attitude is that it is the responsibility of the bank to invest my deposit and pay principal and interest to me at some point in the future.

If I can give my money to the bank without anxiety, can I give God my concerns with equal peace of mind? My answer is an unreserved yes. In practice, it is not always easy just to leave my concerns with God, but with His help I am learning to do it with joy and peace. What about my future? Where will I live? Will I have to suffer my own cooking the rest of my life? What if my health fails? Will I have enough money to live? Life has so many overwhelming worries.

Concerning wages, God can provide my income by allowing me to earn it through employment or by prompting someone to donate money. Either way, He supplies my need. When I dictate to Him the details of what He should do and how and when He should do it, I am in for disappointment. I have found that it is best to let the Father work out the details. "No good thing will he withhold from them that walk uprightly" (Ps. 84:11). He knows what is best. This best includes both the means and the timing. Perhaps if my request is not answered as I wanted, it is because it was not good for me or because I am not walking humbly and uprightly before Him.

As a pastor I have always advised newly widowed people not to make any major decisions in the first year. A griever is in a mentally and emotionally turbulent period of life. In airplane language, this is a time to "return to your seats and fasten your seat belts," a

time to be especially cautious. I realized that I was vulnerable because my mind was unsettled and I was unable to concentrate as
fully as when all was "normal." Almost all major decisions can wait.
When a major decision absolutely must be made, it should be made
only after much prayer and with the counsel of family, friends and,
if necessary, professionals.

In one of my pastorates, a man in his mid-sixties died suddenly
of a heart attack. A few months later, his widow sold the family
home and moved to a larger city a thousand miles away, where a
family member and close friend lived. The widow left behind the
city where she had lived and worked, and the church family and
friends with whom she had fellowshipped for nearly thirty years.
Had she sought my advice, I would not have encouraged such a
drastic move at that time, but I would have encouraged her to
prayerfully give herself time to work through the options.

"Now, preacher, what did *you* do?" you might be asking. At
first, I didn't feel like doing anything about my house and furniture. God knew the state of my troubled mind and heart. Since He
is never in a hurry and never late, I needed to comply with His
timetable. More bad decisions have been made in haste than in
delay. Regarding my house, in the providence of God, Nancy came
along. She wanted a place at the time I was leaving for South Africa. She is a policewoman who capably looked after my house. In
January 1995, I was back in Canada between assignments. David
and I visited our home. Both of us spontaneously agreed that it was
now a house rather than home. With peace of mind, I put our house
up for sale, and it sold quickly in a "down" market. I have since
purchased a condo overlooking a river and a huge park. I'm happy
and have peace about the way the real estate matters have gone.

The discipline of a daily routine has also helped me to adjust.
First I head for the bathroom to shave and get myself spruced up.
Washing and getting dressed make me feel good. Then it is to the
kitchen for a light breakfast, so my stomach stops threatening to
divorce me for lack of support. Next is devotions. I read the por-
tion from the Bible I have set out for the day. (In the early days of
grief, I avidly searched for verses that applied to my specific situation.) There is no substitute for praising and giving thanks to God
for help in grief or any other of life's situations. Prayer follows Bible
reading. In the words of Joseph Scriven,

What a Friend we have in Jesus,
All our sins and griefs to bear!
What a privilege to carry
Ev'rything to God in prayer!
O what peace we often forfeit,
O what needless pain we bear,
All because we do not carry
Ev'rything to God in prayer!

After worshiping God, I am ready to face the day.

One of the best ways to adjust to life is to obey God's explicit and implicit commands. Obedience frees my mind to cope with reordering my life. The man or woman with a clear conscience will not have to expend energy needlessly on justifying sinful behavior or on the sad consequences of his sinful deeds. How would an automatic transmission work if the mechanic did not repair it according to the manufacturer's specifications? If we do things God's way, the "transmission" will work properly. If we are having problems, they may be the result of violating our "manufacturer's manual." Disobeying God adds needless complications to the adjusting process.

Does Jesus care about my success in adjusting? Yes, He cares. I can trust Him with my life, my house, my health and everything else. Jesus' words in Matthew 6:25–34 are a poignant reminder.

Learning to live as a single again after thirty-three years of marriage is not easy. It takes time and planning. I compare it to building a brick structure that needs a carefully laid foundation and good quality mortar and bricks steadily built up one at a time. The foundation represents the Word of God, and the bricks and mortar are the Holy Spirit and prayer. These, together with the loving support of friends, will raise from the ashes of sorrow a ministry with greater depth and dimension.

As a friend of a griever who is adjusting to new reality, please be aware that adjusting is not an easy matter. The loved one will not achieve a successful adjustment in five easy, painless lessons. The griever must work his grief out himself in his own time and unique way. You can help by giving lots of encouragement. Don't laugh too loudly or make a big deal over his blunders. Compliment him and assist him whenever you can, but don't let him become dependent on you. Challenge him to act responsibly and, step by step, to conquer the new reality. Spend time with him. If you are able, give practical help with things he is struggling with, such as pressing his pants or cooking a meal. A little encouragement by word and deed will go a long way in helping your friend adjust.

The Lord has allowed me to be widowed. I want to honor Him in the way I handle my new role. I want to take care of my body and my mind. My worst enemy is myself, I know. God is helping me, giving me peace of mind and a deep sense of purpose for my life. I'm working on shopping, housekeeping, socializing, cooking and a host of other adjustments. Yes, I am getting adjusted to my new lifestyle.

Even though I would like to have a "time out" while I get organized, the old saying is true: "Life goes on." I might like the world to stand still so that I can adjust without interruptions, but life doesn't work like that. My mother used to say, "One must adjust oneself to life and its circumstances." That is what I am trying to do.

11

Combating Loneliness

God hath not promised
*   We shall not know*
Toil and temptation
*   Trouble and woe;*
He hath not told us
*   We shall not bear*
Many a burden,
*   Many a care.*

But God hath promised
*   Strength for the day,*
Rest for the labor,
*   Light for the way,*
Grace for the trials,
*   Help from above,*
Unfailing sympathy,
*   Undying love.*
*   —Annie Johnson Flint*

I don't remember feeling lonely during my youth or marriage, but I have intensely experienced the pangs of loneliness since the accident. Loneliness dogs me, and at times I have a sense of how alone I am. We were created as social beings, and a vacuum exists when we do not have companionship with others. Betty, a young widow in South Africa, told me that many evenings she goes to bed early because she cannot stand another evening at home alone.

Before the accident, I enjoyed an extremely close relationship with my wife and daughter. Suddenly that closeness was gone. I changed from a companionship millionaire to a relationship pauper overnight. I feel as if I have been marooned on a remote Pacific island, cut off from the rest of humanity. I'm lonely because two sources of close, caring human relationships were killed.

I do not feel lonely when I am working, sleeping or watching an exciting game of basketball or football, but I am not always doing those things. The loneliest time for me is bedtime, when my work and relaxation for the day are over and I find myself staring at four blank walls. Closing down for the night and getting ready for bed, I have time to reflect. An empty feeling settles in like an evening mist into a valley. Busyness turns to forlornness. The house becomes so quiet and empty, and my life seems to lose meaning. Bedtime reminds me of learning Greek and Hebrew during seminary days; just "bite the bullet" and hope you will have better days ahead. I can say that with time I've been making progress, and bedtime is not as painful as it once was. I tell the Lord about it as I drift off to sleep.

Besides bedtime, other lonely times include birthdays, anniversaries and holidays. These events just aren't the same without Louise and Ruth. I am not always alone on those occasions; but many times I feel sad, empty and lonely. I am finding that entering into other people's celebrations and rejoicing with those who rejoice drives the blues of loneliness away. Brooding over what I'm missing doesn't improve my lot. I am learning to choose to enjoy the occasions and activities that come my way.

One major area of loneliness is the question Who do I bounce things off now? All of us need to share our concerns, fears, ideas and thoughts with others. Would John Mark have continued in the faith without Barnabas, the encourager, standing with him? As a young child, I shared my hurts, joys and questions with my parents. It's amazing how a big hug and kiss from Mother could dispel many a childhood problem. As I grew older, I began to share "secrets" with a favorite playmate or brother. Later, my confidants were high school and college peers. Finally Louise became my best friend. She listened to my deepest concerns. I did not abandon my mom, dad and friends as counselors, but they took second place to my sweetheart.

Now who do I ask whether my tie is straight? Who will tell me if the hair I have left is combed at the back? Who will point out that my pants need to be pressed or that I am not color-coordinated? Who can give me insight into long-term plans from a woman's perspective? How do I answer a personal, sensitive letter? How should I interpret a particular remark or invitation? Did my sermon fly, or was it a flop? These are not earth-shattering questions, but they all add up to this: I really miss Louise. It's lonely without her input. Louise used to listen to my concerns or "brilliant" ideas. When I would talk about a grandiose scheme and she would just look at me, I knew she wasn't buying it. I would ask her if she thought Mrs. Jones would make a good Sunday School teacher or why John and Mary weren't getting along.

What does a man on his own do to relieve loneliness? We men socialize far less than our women counterparts. I have observed that women will group together to eat, chat or go on vacations. Men are more likely to go off on their own. I remember visiting Kruger National Park in South Africa with Louise in March 1992. We observed two prides of lions. One male lion dominates each pride consisting of three to seven females and their offspring. The females socialize as a group. After a few years a new male challenger expels the older male lion from the pride. The old male lion wanders the forest alone. At times I feel like that expelled male lion. I covet another human being with whom to share conversation and companionship. I feel a great need to share my ideas with spiritually mature friends. Slowly and sensitively, I share personal thoughts with a small group of trustworthy friends. Some aspects of my life I share only with the Lord. But I also recognize the need for human contact to prevent being labeled crazy, always talking to myself.

Planning and action are necessary to combat loneliness. What are some of the ways I use? Let me tell you about one Saturday. At 8:00 A.M. I went to a men's breakfast meeting and enjoyed the fellowship. Afterward some friends came over for a short visit. I washed and vacuumed my car and went for a brisk walk. I had planned to go out with some people for supper, but that plan was canceled at the last minute; so I telephoned Joe, a fellow widower, to see what he was doing. He already had made plans to see family members. It was too late for me to make other supper arrangements. The refrigerator was low in food, so I had cereal for supper. It was a lonely evening, but I chose not to sit around feeling sad and miserable. I got busy trying to finish a project on my computer. To make up for the lack of other social contact, I telephoned some family members and friends.

For me the most helpful way to alleviate loneliness is to become involved with other people. I don't want to be a nuisance, but I am seeking to contribute to their lives. What fun the children have been! Seven-year-old Marc in Cape Town is the special target of my gentle teasing about being chased by girls. Older couples sometimes do not have their own family nearby and are rich sources of companionship. They help me, and I trust that I encourage them. I certainly enjoy their fellowship and our times together. Fellowship times are more than mere social contact. The point of spending time with people is not entertainment—after all, even the most captivating person would eventually become boring—but contribution to each others' lives. I want to give myself to others, whether or not they, in turn, minister to me. When we love and obey the Lord Jesus and love and serve others, we receive great joy in our hearts. The world puts self first and others second, and Jesus is seldom thought of at all. Spelling "J-O-Y" as "Jesus, Others and You," as the old song says, is the pathway to real joy.

I have also tried new activities with friends, such as going to the opera, attending a cricket match and eating Indian and Afrikaans food. These activities are mere substitutes for the rich companionship I once enjoyed with my wife and daughter; but they provide social fellowship, and they drive away some of the clouds of loneliness. I'm trying to be creative in finding new ways to be involved with people socially. Also I am finding I am able to be alone without feeling miserable or fidgety. Sometimes I have a sense of freedom knowing I can blare the music or keep the light on without disturbing anyone. At other times I just enjoy the silence.

As a friend, encourage the griever to keep busy at his work, play and, very importantly, with other people doing things together. You can help immensely by sharing your life and your family's life with him. These events don't have to be expensive, just things you or your family are doing: a barbecue, a picnic, a long walk, cross-country skiing, a game or whatever. Put yourself in the griever's shoes. What activities would you like? Discuss the possibilities and make plans to get together with your friends regularly.

Friends! How could I have managed without them? Virtually every week during the two postings in South Africa since the accident, one friend has sent me a letter and another a fax. What an antidote to loneliness! Other friends have sat with me, wept with me, fed me and shown their love in innumerable ways, big and small. They telephoned, sent flowers for no special reason, invited me to their homes for an evening out. I thank God for all these people; but in times of deep loneliness, I throw myself into the comforting arms of my Heavenly Father. I am compelled to rely on God for my emotional sustenance and survival.

Like King David in Psalm 31, I have found the Lord is my fortress for survival. David faced adversity because Saul persistently sought to kill him. Imagine David's emotional and psychological state under such incredible stress. Was he bitter, depressed or vengeful? David's circumstances, while vastly different from mine, prompted him to write about themes that strike a responsive cord in me. Like David, I need to keep my eyes on God and His "marvellous kindness," not on my sad circumstances. David issues a challenge to all who love the Lord and hope in Him: Be courageous. He invites us to know experientially that the Lord preserves the faithful. He reminds us that God strengthens the weak. Loneliness comes, but God is my fortress against it.

12

Dating and Relating to Others

*O, the comfort—the inexpressible comfort of feeling
safe with a person.
Having neither to weigh thoughts,
Nor measure words—but pouring them right out—
just as they are—
Chaff and grain together,
Certain that a faithful hand will take and shift
them—
Keep what is worth keeping—
And with the breath of kindness blow the rest away.*
—Friendship, *by Dinah Craik*

I remember when I was a youngster at grade school: the older boys would choose two softball captains, who in turn would select their teams. As a younger boy, I would stand on the edge of the group hoping to be selected, often to become the last boy chosen for a team. I was happy to be playing, but I felt sad that I was permitted to play only on the captain's sufferance.

At first as a single again, I had the same feeling when I was

83

invited to social functions. I was happy to have been invited, but I felt I had been asked only because the host and hostess took pity on me. I was wrong for thinking that, but I did feel out of place because everyone else had a spouse.

For me, reentering singleness after thirty-three years of marriage was like being told, "Tonight we are not watching the Dallas Cowboys and Washington Redskins play football, but England and Australia play cricket." There is a distinct difference, and I definitely prefer football.

While Louise was alive, our social world was made up almost exclusively of couples. I had known Louise for almost thirty-five years, first dating her and then being a married couple. Suddenly I was thrust into a world for which I was not prepared. I felt nervous among couples. How did I fit in without Louise? I still felt married to her, even though she was gone. Would my married friends try to marry me off now that I was "fair game"? Was it intrusive of me to talk to a married woman, as if I were usurping her husband's right to her company? Would my chatting with a married buddy anger his wife because I was invading her time with him? I was extremely reluctant to keep husbands and wives apart for even the briefest moment of time, thinking, *What if this is their last chance to speak with each other?* With the passing of time, I grew less frantic and loosened up considerably. I realized my spending a few minutes talking with a husband would not upset his wife. Rarely do couples experience the tragic loss of a spouse the way I did. They will not begrudge my ten-minute conversation with a good friend. Nor will a spouse resent my chatting with his or her partner.

In the early days of my newly found singleness, I was uptight around any single woman who was even remotely close to my age. I had a deaf ear to matchmakers; and if any woman made advances, I took no notice. (There are some advantages to not being good looking or wealthy.) I certainly had not chosen to be single, but neither was I so desperate not to be alone that I was looking for an immediate replacement. As time passed, I became less threatened in the presence of single women. I am more at peace with myself and am learning to treat all women as friends.

Before and after the accident, I heard people who had lost a spouse say, "I never thought of dating," or "I never dreamed of remarrying." Interestingly, these comments almost always came from widowed people who are now remarried. What happened? How did each of them magically transform from blessed single-ness to blissful marriage? The impression they give is that they never even thought of a possible new romantic relationship. Then like a meteor out of the midnight sky, a new Mr. or Mrs. Right appeared, and the professed hard-liner melted like a snowball on the equator. Did Mr. or Mrs. "I Never Thought of Dating" really never think of dating, or did he or she say that because it is per-ceived as the proper response? Take it one step further. My friend Lucille, who after the death of her husband "never had one thought of remarrying," has now remarried and is praying daily that I find a wife. (Maybe you would pray for me, too, if you saw my house-keeping and cooking!)

As a widower, is something wrong with me if I meet an attrac-tive-to-me single Christian woman, somewhat compatible with me, and I think that one day she might be a possible date? As of this writing, more than two years after the accident, I have not yet dated. That fact does not mean I have not thought about dating. I have. I don't feel guilty about this line of thought. I do not find any Bibli-cal, moral or ethical prohibition to dating someone of the opposite sex. My marriage to Louise was "until death do us part." I antici-pated that we would grow old together. I never expected that she would precede me so soon in death. While I may never remarry, the possibility exists. Remarriage would speak well of my former marriage in which I was both happy and fulfilled. I am neither fos-tering lustful thinking nor actively seeking a wife. But should God so direct, I am willing to consider the possibility without feeling guilty. If marriage should occur, it will come about after prayer and counsel. I do not readily discuss this matter, lest I be misunder-stood as a woman-chaser or be thought disloyal to Louise.

The Bible does not forbid remarriage after the death of a spouse. As a Christian, one may in good conscience remarry another Chris-tian. When? Scripture doesn't spell out a time frame, but that does not mean one can or should begin a new relationship immediately after the end of the previous one. Common sense and cultural or psychological implications need to be taken into consideration. Western Church culture and tradition seem to indicate that a "rea-sonable" lapse of time between relationships is at least one year. A new relationship started just months after the death of a spouse is viewed as a lack of respect for the former spouse. We need to bear in mind the views of Christian brothers and sisters and seek to avoid giving offense in this matter.

Seven or eight months after Louise's death, I was psychologically nowhere near ready to begin a new relationship. I felt as if I were functioning well but was keenly aware that I was not mentally free from my relationship with Louise. The wounds were still tender, and I was almost constantly thinking about her, wondering what we would be doing if she were still alive. Trying to fulfill my ministry while experiencing flashbacks to former days exhausted me. Even if I had wanted to, I was unable to put the time and energy into developing a new relationship.

Trying to start a new relationship before I am mentally and emotionally ready would be disastrous. It would be unfair to any woman and selfish on my part. I am unable to walk in two directions at the same time. In the professional football world, an injured player must wait until he is fully recovered from his injuries before returning to the gridiron, or he risks being easily injured again. In the world of relationships, it is unwise to develop a new romance until the hurts and pains of the former relationship are healed. I must wait for the Lord to direct me. Scheming, plotting or setting my own timetable for a new relationship would be detrimental to both of us.

Dr. Wendell Kempton, president of ABWE, stayed with me during the early days of my grief. Having lost his first wife suddenly in 1980, he knew so well what I was going through. We wept and prayed together. He shared precious, private thoughts. Most of all, he listened. Fellow Canadian Mel Cuthbert also gave advice and caution. Both men spoke from their experience of suddenly losing their beloved wives. They know the shock, sorrow, loneliness and temptations of men whose wives have died.

Men are in a particularly precarious position as newly made singles. We are accustomed to married life with its physical pleasures. We have been created with a sexual drive, although the death of a spouse dampens this drive. My sexual feelings were not eradicated, although this dampening of desire is quite common for some time following the death. However, these sexual feelings were highly offensive to me in my recovery.

Men who are alone desperately need companionship and can

easily succumb to filling that need outside the will of God. Unfortunately, some women can be quite forward. And while God stated in Genesis 2:18, "It is not good that the man should be alone," we must be alert for potential trouble spots and act according to Biblical principles at all times. Satan wants to take advantage of us in our weaknesses, but I know that "greater is he that is in you, than he that is in the world" (1 John 4:4).

Fantasizing about sex is dangerous at any time. In the loneliness of another solitary evening, it is easy for the mind to drift. We can slowly start down the tantalizing road of sexual thought and rapidly find ourselves "off limits." Jesus warned, "Whosoever looketh on a woman to lust after her hath committed adultery with her already in his heart" (Matt. 5:28). Martin Luther supposedly said that one may not be able to prevent birds from flying over his head, but he does not have to let them build a nest in his hair. A thought may come into our minds, but we do not have to feed and water it: we can order it out. We must remember, ". . . Whatsoever things are true, whatsoever things are honest, whatsoever things are just, whatsoever things are pure, whatsoever things are lovely, whatsoever things are of good report; if there be any virtue, and if there be any praise, think on these things" (Phil. 4:8).

God ordained when and with whom our sexual functions may have expression—between a man and a woman who are married to each other. The marriage relationship is among the most blessed and mutually beneficial of God's gifts to mankind. When the relationship is broken through death, this beautiful gift has to be set aside. Grieving demands giving one's full attention to becoming whole again. Sin against God and others impedes the healing process. On the other hand, within the boundaries of God's Word and at the right time, new relationships can be developed in love and respect for our good and His glory.

As time passed, I realized that people began to be bold in their teasing me about my single state. Surprisingly men were worse about this than their matchmaking wives. A word of caution: resist the temptation to make flippant remarks about dating and remarriage.

As a friend of a griever, you can help by daily and earnestly praying privately for the grieving one. If you see a relationship starting and red warning signals flash in your mind, without delay and with great sensitivity express your concerns to your friend. He or she doesn't need a second broken heart. Carefully pick the correct time, then tactfully mention that you are available to prayerfully discuss with him the matter of remarriage. Then promise that you will keep your lips sealed. Encourage your friend to build on his present relationships and/or to develop new friendships that are healthy and wholesome. There is nothing wrong with a new relationship in God's will, in God's way and in God's time.

13

Accepting Death

Amy Carmichael, a missionary to India, eloquently listed the ways people attempt to cope with the unexplainable. Some try forgetting; some fill their lives with work; others remain aloof from the events that threaten to overwhelm them. Still others blindly submit to fate. She closed a poem with these forceful words:

> He said, "I will accept the breaking sorrow
> Which God tomorrow
> Will to His son explain."
> Then did the turmoil deep within him cease.
>
> Not vain the word, not vain;
> *For in acceptance lieth peace.*

The major components of accepting death are both knowing

and believing the Scriptures. God's Word provides the theological bedrock on which to build an acceptance of death. Without such a foundation I would have been driven hither and yon by the winds of doubt, emotion and the opinions of men.

After receiving the news of the accident, I remembered the life of Job. Behind the scenes and without Job's knowledge, a battle was being fought. Job was the focal point of a discussion between God and Satan. God allowed Satan to hammer Job to prove that he would not curse God even under the most desperate of circumstances. In one day Job lost all his wealth, his servants and animals and, most precious of all, his seven sons and three daughters. He experienced a degree of loss that few other human beings have ever sustained.

"Then Job arose, and [tore] his mantle, and shaved his head, and fell down upon the ground, and worshipped, and said, . . . the LORD gave, and the LORD hath taken away; blessed be the name of the LORD. In all this Job sinned not, nor charged God foolishly" (Job 1:20–22).

Not only did Job tear his robe and shave his head as his culture demanded, but he also "fell to the ground and worshipped." His thoughts turned from personal loss to the Creator "from whom all blessings flow." Job might have looked around him at the waves of circumstances that could easily have drown him in depression. Instead, Job focused on God and acknowledged His lordship. His emotions crushed, Job still turned his eyes to the Lord and tenaciously maintained his spiritual integrity.

When I look at the world today, I see death, disease, violence, corruption, immorality and broken lives and hearts. When I look to God, I find hope, meaning and peace. In my times of deepest hurt and sorrow, the words of Job rang in my heart. In the Psalms and other Scripture passages, I read promises that diminished my losses as I turned from my situation to worship the Lord. Worship is a most effective prescription for tragedy. Worship focuses a person's attitude on God.

"The LORD gave." We all like to receive gifts. James 1:17 declares, "Every good gift and every perfect gift is from above, and cometh down from the Father. . . ." My wife and daughter were gifts from God. The words "the LORD gave" point out that even life is on loan from God. I have use of the gifts He has given me for a short period of time. I tend to forget this fact and become possessive. God has given His Son and so much more to me; I have given little back to Him in comparison. "Thank You, Lord, for all Your gifts."

"The LORD hath taken away." To the degree that it is wonderful to receive, it is equally hard to give anything up. My all-wise Heavenly Father has seen fit to take my wife and daughter into His presence. Since He created and redeemed them, He has every right to receive them into Heaven whenever and however He chooses. I know He has in mind what is best for me, even though I cannot fully understand how it is best. I thank Him for the part I was allowed to share in their lives.

"Blessed be the name of the LORD." I moved from worship to praise and thanksgiving. In blessing God, I acknowledged who He is and the divine gifts He has bestowed to me. Blessing God is not contingent upon what happens to me, but is centered on the character, attributes and goodness of God. The Lord gave. The Lord has taken away. The Lord is to be blessed at all times, including times of sorrow.

How was I going to apply this truth intellectually and emotionally to Louise's and Ruth's deaths? Intellectually I had no problem. Emotionally, I was sitting on a raw nerve. My attitude stayed positive because I knew in my heart of hearts that "as for God, his way is perfect" (Ps. 18:30). Everything God does is perfect. I could not explain the whys and wherefores, but my trusting attitude helped immensely in accepting the deaths of my loved ones. Romans 12:2 affirms that the will of God is good, acceptable and perfect.

During my little speech at our wedding reception, I quoted from James 1:17 and applied the words to Louise: "Every perfect gift is from above." Louise often teased me about my remarks in reference to my "perfect" wife. What she did, she did exceedingly well indeed; but in comparison to Jesus she, like all of us, fell far short of His perfection.

Louise was a perfectionist. The tablecloth had to hang exactly the same length on each side of the table. God is not a perfectionist. He *is* perfect. If there are tablecloths in the mansions in my Father's house, they are hanging perfectly. Imagine everything being perfect and being done perfectly. Imagine everyone being perfect. In this world, forget it. But rejoice! God is perfect, and all that He does is perfect.

Since God is perfect, then the Home-going of His children fits perfectly into His timetable. Our timetables have us scheduled to live well into our eighties at the very least. John "the beloved" disciple lived to an unusually old age and died of natural causes, yet his brother James was killed as a young man at the order of King Herod. Peter died as a martyr, yet God did not permit Satan to take Job's life. Solomon wrote, "[There is] a time to be born, and a time to die" (Eccles. 3:2).

I picture God weaving a huge, beautiful tapestry out of my life. I can see only the underside of the tapestry with all kinds of threads hanging down, and I cannot make out much of a pattern. But one day I will see the finished tapestry and marvel at its beauty. I will see the design, the tiny specks of silver and the black borders that are just as much a part of the design as the broad strands of blue. I do not understand all His ways, but I do know that "His ways are perfect."

The strong emotional cords that bound me to my wife and daughter were not severed with their deaths, but death did bring an immediate end to our human relationship. Because of our strong and loving ties, their loss is even more painful than it would have been otherwise. That loss is the price to be paid for enjoying fulfilling relationships. Yet I am learning to accept their absence.

In accepting death, I am being freed to begin to grow again in a special closeness to Jesus. Our Lord was sent

> To heal the brokenhearted, . . .
> To comfort all who mourn, . . .
> To give them beauty for ashes,
> The oil of joy for mourning,
> The garment of praise for the spirit of heaviness . . .
> —(Isa. 61:1–3, NKJV)

I have asked Him to do these acts of love in my heart, and day by day He does!

As a friend of a griever you cannot accept death theologically or philosophically on behalf of your friend. You might be able to answer some of his questions or direct him to someone else. But most likely, his questions cannot be answered. You can, however, be a loving, caring friend who is there through thick and thin. You can encourage him by word and example to seek God and walk with Him as never before. You can pray specifically that God would grant him that peace that passes all human understanding.

Make sure your loved one is studying the Scriptures. Applying the Word of God is the only basis for accepting death. The refrain of an old hymn rings true:

> We have an anchor that keeps the soul
> Steadfast and sure while the billows roll,
> Fastened to the Rock which cannot move,
> Grounded firm and deep in the Savior's love.

14

A Year Later

When all is done, say not my day is o'er
And that through night I seek a dimmer shore;
Say rather that my morn has just begun.
I greet the dawn and not a setting sun,
When all is done.

—John O. Means

Throughout the first year after the deaths of my wife and daughter, I experienced God's grace to help me walk through the process of grief. Slowly but steadily, I could see that I was healing. I had a few glitches, but I was satisfied with my progression toward a new normalcy. I was looking less and less at the past and more and more toward the future. In April 1994 I completed my interim ministry at Everglen Baptist Church in Cape Town, South Africa. I flew home to Canada planning to return to Durban, South Africa, for another short-term ministry on July 1, 1994. But before leaving Canada I had to face the first anniversary of the accident.

I had scheduled a five-week speaking tour on Canada's East Coast, partly because my tour had been interrupted by the accident the year before. Anniversary day would fall while I was there. I was anticipating and dreading it at the same time. It hung like an ominous cloud in the distance. I was billeted for Saturday, May 14, at the Millers' home near Halifax, Nova Scotia. That was where I had learned of the accident. I felt uneasy as I recalled the events surrounding the breaking of the news the previous year, but that uneasiness was merely a squall before the storm.

I preached twice on Sunday, May 15, and each evening through Thursday. I was so busy I had no time to think about the upcoming anniversary. On Friday, I caught a ferry to picturesque Prince Edward Island, where I was to speak at a missionary banquet on Saturday evening and at the Sunday morning service.

Saturday, May 22, was anniversary day, both the first anniversary of the accident and Louise's and my thirty-fourth wedding anniversary. The day was gorgeous, with new life bursting everywhere. I had the flu but tried to carry on with business as usual. I went for a long walk in the sunshine. As I passed a cemetery, the storm broke over me. Thinking about Louise and Ruth and of the many events and experiences we had shared, I found pain and loss overtaking me. I mourned the loss of their great potential. I wondered what we would be doing if they were alive that day. I relived their deaths and the funeral. I reviewed the great emotional pain and adjustment I had experienced during the past year. I examined the ongoing reorganization and rebuilding of my life. Even as I brought to mind all those memories, I surprised myself by realizing that the storm of grief was less intense.

One regret that has deeply distressed me is the suddenness of their deaths. If I had been able to close off our relationship, I would not have had such a sinking feeling. Being able to say "good-bye" would have made the grieving process easier.

Back from my walk, I telephoned Victoria to talk to my son, David, for about thirty minutes. We relived days gone by: church and school functions, trips, vacations, birthdays and Christmases. We speculated on what might have been and asked each other how we were doing. Talking to David was therapeutic for me at the lowest point of that day. David and I were one in sorrow as we poured out our thoughts in total empathy. We agreed to talk later to review how the day had progressed for each of us. My cup of grief had been poured out; it was time to refill it with hope.

The missionary banquet on Prince Edward Island that evening brought an unexpected treat. Art and Jean Bell were Air Force personnel and at one time members of Louise's home church. They also had been guests at our wedding. I had lost track of them, so it was a wonderful surprise to see them after more than thirty years. The Lord was gracious to provide old friends in a new-to-me church. I found it difficult to smile, but my slide/tape presentation and message were well received by the congregation.

The dark clouds of that first anniversary stayed with me for several weeks. In some ways, it was like a second funeral without the intensity of the original. But once again I had to weather the reminiscing, loss and pain that the anniversary stirred up. Anniversaries, birthdays and Christmases will come and go, and I will always experience the sharp flashback of memories. Like the scar on the middle finger of my right hand, the scar of memory will always be there, and I will live with it.

May I make a suggestion to those who are trying to help their grieving friends? At the anniversary of the death, do not say, "Oh, this must be a horrible time for you. Your dear Tom (or Mary or whoever) died. How terrible!" In fact, do not even raise the subject at anniversary time. If the griever does so, that is a different story. Then, in a very natural way, try to do something together. Don't make it overly obvious so that, instead of bringing joy, the occasion causes your friend to relive and highlight the death, pain and loss.

As the days passed, I found myself wondering how well I had reacted over the past year and how well I was reacting presently. I had declared many times, "It's not what happens to you; it's how you react that counts." I had to practice what I had preached. I have carefully analyzed Job's words, "Though he slay me, yet will I trust in him" (Job 13:15). It is easy to quote this verse when things are going smoothly. It was after the dust of sorrow had settled that I could meaningfully reaffirm Job's words to God. How I respond to Him sets the tone of the attitude I show to others. If my vertical response (to God) is correct, my horizontal response (before others) will be also.

How have I responded to my trial? A greater fear of the Lord has settled in my soul like a blanket of new snow. I have experienced a greater awe of God and, at the same time, an increased sense of my own unworthiness. I know that many people are observing my responses and reactions, and I do not want to fail God as a poor role model. Since the accident, I have had the uncanny feeling that I am being observed both by those who know me well and by those who only know of me.

The challenge to respond properly drives me to allow God's Spirit to control my thoughts and actions. Submitting to His control is far better than trying to run things myself. Running things myself is apt to end in failure. I pray, "Lord, help me not to grab the steering wheel out of Your hands." I am consciously evaluating and reevaluating the manner in which my reactions impact others. To paraphrase the words of Paul, I am stretching every muscle to its limit, beating my body into subjection as I press toward the goal of winning the spiritual Olympics. If I want to triumph, I must be willing to train, work hard and persevere.

In considering my personal attitudes and actions and how they impact others, I was reminded of Paul's words in 2 Corinthians 3:2: "Ye are our epistle written in our hearts, known and read of all men." In our world, the Bible most people read is not the King James Version or the New International Version, but you and me. People carefully scrutinize our attitudes, words and deeds. Can those people clearly see Jesus in me? Our neighbors, fellow workers and extended family members are not blind or indifferent to the "Bible" of our lives. They are watching, especially when they know we are facing a battle. Are they reading in me a better way than they know to handle life and death? My concern about people's reading me has challenged me to examine what I am telling others through my life. This challenge moves me away from thinking so much about myself to thinking about Jesus and others.

At the one-year point, it seemed to me as if the accident had happened only yesterday, yet it also seemed an eternity ago. I thank God for all the people who have prayed for me and helped me in innumerable ways. God is so good. In April 1994, I was visiting our mission offices in Pennsylvania and was introduced to a couple. They looked at me in disbelief and confided in me, "We heard of you, and we pray for you regularly. We can't believe we're actually meeting you." That conversation is an example of how the first year went.

God has done so much for me. I want to praise Him with these words, "Now unto him that is able to do exceedingly abundantly above all that we ask or think, according to the power that worketh in us, unto him be glory in the church by Christ Jesus throughout all ages, world without end. Amen" (Eph. 3:20, 21).

15

Claiming the Victory

*I am standing upon the seashore; a ship at my side
     spreads
her white sails to the morning breeze and starts for the
     blue ocean.
She is an object of beauty and strength and I stand
and watch her until at length she hangs like a speck of
     white cloud
just where the sea and sky come to mingle with each other.
Then someone at my side says, "There! She's gone."*

*Gone where? Gone from my sight—that is all.
She is just as large in mast and hull and spar
as she was when she left my side
and just as able to bear her load of living freight to the
     place of destination.
Her diminished size is in me, not in her;
and just at the moment when someone at my side says,
"There! She's gone"—
there are other eyes watching her coming
and other voices ready to take up the glad shout,
"There she comes!"*

. . . and that is dying.   —*Author Unknown*

Right from the time of the accident, I resolved by God's grace that although I had been hit hard by the recent events in my life, I was going to master my situation. I was determined to rebuild my shattered life and with joy carry on my missionary work. At the funeral I thanked the attendees for their love and prayers and told them I would be returning to South Africa as soon as I could get the details of my life straightened out. I did return. I have completed a number of six- or eight-month assignments in Durban and Cape Town, and plans are underway for me to be the interim missionary pastor in other places.

As I write these words two years after the deaths, the accident is still unreal to me. At times I shake my head and pinch myself to make sure I am not dreaming. Occasionally spasms of sorrow still flash across my mind like lightning. But the skies soon clear, and I am back to my new "normal." I miss Louise and Ruth terribly, but I do not wish them back in this cruel world. The apostle Paul wrote,

"For I reckon that the sufferings of this present time are not worthy to be compared with the glory which shall be revealed in us" (Rom. 8:18). I am happy that they are enjoying perfect peace and bliss. I envy them. I wonder if Ruth has a red sports car to whip around the streets of gold. Humanly speaking, I could have twenty-five more years before I see them again. In the light of 100 trillion years and eternity barely begun, the next twenty-five years here will seem as a raindrop in the Pacific Ocean. Beyond that stands the realization that Jesus Christ might come today.

Paul looked expectantly toward Christ's return. His life was not easy. We read that he was

. . . in labours more abundant, in stripes above measure, in prisons more frequent, in deaths oft. Of the Jews five times received I forty stripes save one. Thrice was I beaten with rods, once was I stoned, thrice I suffered shipwreck, a night and a day I have been in the deep; in journeyings often, in perils of waters, in perils of robbers, in perils by mine own countrymen, in perils by the heathen, in perils in the city, in perils in the wilderness, in perils in the sea, in perils among false brethren; in weariness and painfulness, in watchings often, in hunger and thirst, in fastings often, in cold and nakedness. Beside those things that are without, that which cometh upon me daily, the care of all the churches (2 Cor. 11:23–28).

Paul responded to all the negatives in his life in the words of Romans 8:37: "Yet in all these things we are more than conquerors through Him who loved us" (NKJV). In spite of every possible horrible happening and circumstance, Paul stated emphatically that absolutely nothing could separate him—or us—from the love of God.

If we lose everything but have God, we have everything; if we have everything but don't have God, we are grasping the wind. I can lose my wife and daughter, my health, my pension fund, my country and freedom, my pleasures and more, but I cannot be separated from God's love. So if I take a major hit, it is not the end of my world. I have God. Why would I mope around in self-pity or let anger and bitterness grow in my heart? God has called me to live for Him. God loves me and has gifted me as a missionary pastor/teacher. I have important work to do. I have been immensely blessed.

After Paul was stoned and left for dead at Lystra, he got up, dusted himself off and went right back to his missionary work. That is what I did also. At the end of his life, the apostle Paul was able to say, "I have fought the good fight, I have finished the race, I have kept the faith" (2 Tim. 4:7, NKJV). My heart's desire is to be able to say those words, too, when my time of departure comes.

In recent years Louise's favorite verse was Romans 8:28: "And we know that all things work together for good to them that love God. . . ." I am sure that today she is dancing around Heaven affirming, "All things work together for good." Maybe she now knows that she missed dying following an agonizing struggle with cancer. She had had two mastectomies, one in 1978 and another in 1991, but she was steadfast and victorious in spirit through both surgeries. Louise used those dehumanizing procedures to witness of the grace and strength God gives in trials. She had victory. She turned the operations into opportunities to minister to the spiritual and emotional needs of other women who experienced or anticipated similar operations. She used her adversities for the good of others. She not only quoted the verse; she also lived it.

We find it hard to understand how negative events can "work together for good." We see death, sickness, injury, financial loss, defeat, injustice and waste as tragedies. In a human sense, they are. But who promised that this life would always be rosy? Murder, violence, rape, war, stealing, abuse and other violations of God's commandments are part of life in this world. Sometimes those who love God are victims who suffer. "Why did God allow this tragedy to happen to His dear child?" we ask. I do not know why, but I do know that God works all things together for good to those who love Him. All I can do is remain faithful to God and His promises and look for ways to turn evil into good.

Adversities often reveal areas in my character that need improvement. My positive reaction to a negative event can help me become more like Christ. If I become more loving, courteous, patient, tolerant, kind, faithful and peaceable and have greater self-control, I am making progress toward becoming like Jesus. If I don't become bitter when unfortunate events occur, God can use even the hurtful things to develop my character for my good and for His glory. Then the adversity becomes the motivation for change and new gains in my Christian life. This is victory!

A few days after the funeral, I was reading in 2 Corinthians 1:3 and 4 about the ". . . God of all comfort; who comforteth us in all our tribulation, that we may be able to comfort them which are in any trouble, by the comfort wherewith we ourselves are comforted of God." The thought flashed across my mind, *You will have a new dimension of ministry.* I knew it was true, but at the time it did not seem that I would ever be able to comfort anyone. When I returned to Cape Town and was reviewing the church directory with one of the leaders, he pointed to a name and said, "Some time back this family lost two daughters in a car accident." Coincidence? No. The door of opportunity was looking me right in the eye. *By your grace, Lord, I will try to share with others the comfort You have given me.*

Notice the word "that" in 2 Corinthians 1:4. God's express purpose in helping us is so *that* we can minister to others. We are comforted so that we in turn can give comfort and help to others. Who better to console a mastectomy victim than another mastectomy patient? Who better to comfort a widow than another widow? Who better to minister to one who has lost his job to corporate restructuring than one who has had the same experience?

I have known God's comfort and help. My troubles are not in vain when I use the experience to lighten the burdens of similarly needy people. I must not keep the blessings to myself but must glorify our Lord by helping others. We are partners with God in administering comfort. I want to go with His help and tell others how He has helped me through troubles.

If the tragedy of losing my wife and daughter had not occurred, I would not have been offered certain opportunities to speak of God's love, power and salvation. I once conducted a funeral where another person would normally have delivered the message. I preached the way of salvation to people I am reasonably certain would otherwise never have heard a clear explanation of how to have a personal relationship with Jesus Christ. My experience opened that door. Another time, a pastor asked me to accompany him to visit a family who had lost their twenty-three-year-old daughter to a brain aneurysm. The pastor affirmed that, because of my experience, I ministered to those people on a level he could not.

Sharing what God has done for me has brought a wealth of blessing for me and has opened opportunities to tell others of God's grace in my life. I have been able to give encouragement, with understanding, to a Christian brother who lost his wife to cancer. I have spent time praying with and consoling grandparents whose twenty-one-year-old grandson died from a heart attack while he was out jogging. I talked to a couple whose five-year-old son was crushed to death against a tree by a neighbor's pickup. I empathized with a World War II war bride who lost her husband of almost fifty years. At an airport, I was able to communicate my faith in Jesus Christ with a woman whose life was in shambles. When she asked how I coped, I was able to tell her about the accident and direct her to the One who is our all. I referred her to a good local church. Only eternity will reveal the impact of these many opportunities.

I have been able to challenge other people to use their experiences of God's help in times of trouble. Kathy, a businesswoman who attends my church in South Africa, came bursting into Bible study one Wednesday night full of excitement. "Pastor Wally, after you challenged us on Sunday, a man came into my shop and started talking about a problem I, too, have faced. I was able to explain to him how God helped me. Isn't that great?"

Kathy is a relatively new Christian who has never had formal Bible training. But she is able to tell from personal experience what God has done in her life. I know I am blessed as I help others go through trials like mine and challenge people like Kathy to use her experience to help others. If God has helped you, look around; you will find others to whom you can minister comfort and help. With our submission to God and His help, what looks like tragedy and defeat in our lives can bring hope and victory to many others.

I am deeply humbled to hear that my life has been a challenging inspiration to others to follow the Lord. My triumph in trials is not something of myself; it is the result of God's grace and help to me. If anyone has been helped through me, I praise God.

My son, David, expressed a triumphant hope in a poem he wrote in July 1995:

> Like flowers cut, not left to die
> They've made their home up in the sky.
> And someday in the by-and-by
> We'll meet again.

Until that day, we'll shed a tear
Remembering that our dreams lie here.

I stayed one evening at a bed-and-breakfast operated by a Christian couple. Our conversation turned to my trying to write this book. The lady expressed an interest in reading it, so I gave her what I had written thus far. When I walked into the dining room the following morning, she was seated at the table in tears, reading the manuscript. She cried, "This is so helpful." My sincere prayer is that my personal story might be a genuine help and inspiration to fellow mourners.

Looking back over my life, I realize that the accident was not the greatest or pivotal event of my life. Another surpasses it and has dominated the course of my life. I was reared in a good family and was baptized as an infant. I considered myself a Christian. I certainly had a religion but not a relationship with God. I did not know God personally or experientially. While growing up, I often wondered about God and the meaning and purpose of life. These subjects troubled me, but I dismissed them and went on with life.

After high school I entered the working world, which soon lost its glitter. At that time I found a New Testament in our home. Reading it, I understood that God is holy and I am not. I shared my concerns with a fellow worker, who gave good counsel. With virtually no knowledge of theology but with a seeking heart, I simply cried out to God to make me a real Christian. He did, and my life began to change. God established a personal relationship between us on the basis of my repentance and faith. That relationship has grown and deepened as we have faced the ups and downs of life together.

My old Christian life reminds me of an oak veneer table. It might look all right to me, but under the veneer is just pressed cardboard. There is no depth or substance to it. My new Christian life reminds me of a solid oak table. It's real. God is real and personal to me now. The Scriptures are now part of my daily life. My faith can triumphantly meet the tests and trials of life because it is solid at the core. May I ask about you? Do you simply have a religion, or do you have a real relationship with God through personal faith in Jesus Christ? I urge you to consider this matter, confess your sin and through faith believe in the Lord Jesus Christ.

I brought nothing into this world, and I will be taking nothing of material value out with me. It would be tragic if I got so involved with the issues and "toys" of this life that I neglected the real issue of life: my relationship with God. My worship and service of God is paramount in my life. I find that I continually have to fight self and this world's detractions so that I can keep the main thing the main thing in my life. When I leave this life, whether by death or by Christ's return, only my faith and the record of what I have done for Jesus will leave with me. My AST computer, my Tilley hat and my autographed Blue Jay baseball are staying on this planet. When I stand before God and He looks over my record, I want to hear, "Well done, Wally. You have been a good and faithful servant." That declaration is the ultimate victory and reward.

"Now thanks be unto God, which always causeth us to triumph in Christ, and maketh manifest the savour of his knowledge by us in every place" (2 Cor. 2:14).

If you have experienced tragedy in your life and wish to correspond with the author, here is the address to use:

Rev. Wally Stephenson
ABWE
P.O. Box 8585
Harrisburg, PA 17105-8585